MW00989762

LANDLORD/TENANT RIGHTS IN WASHINGTON

Sidney J. Strong, Attorney

Self-Counsel Press Inc.
a subsidiary of
International Self-Counsel Press Ltd.

Printed in Canada

First edition: June 1977
Second edition: November 1979
Third edition: March 1982
Fourth edition: September 1984
Fifth edition: November 1986
Sixth edition: March 1989
Seventh edition: September 1990
Eighth edition: January 1993; Reprinted: April 1996
Ninth edition: July 1999

Cataloging in Publication Data

Strong, Sidney J., 1942-
  Landlord/tenant rights in Washington

  (Self-counsel legal series)
  ISBN 1-55180-255-4

  1. Landlord and tenant — Washington (State) — Popular Works.   I. Title.   II. Series.
KFW117.Z9S8 1999   346.79704'34   C99-910674-0

Self-Counsel Press Inc.
1704 N. State Street
Bellingham, Washington 98225
a subsidiary of
International Self-Counsel Press Ltd.
1481 Charlotte Road
North Vancouver, British Columbia
Canada V7J 1H1

CONTENTS

SAMPLES

NOTICE TO READERS

Laws are constantly changing. Every effort is made to keep this publication as current as possible. However, the author, the publisher, and the vendor of this book make no representation or warranties regarding the outcome or the use to which the information in this book is put and are not assuming any liability for any claims, losses, or damages arising out of the use of this book. The reader should not rely on the author or the publisher of this book for any professional advice. Please be sure that you have the most recent edition.

INTRODUCTION

This book is more a clinical study of the Residential Landlord-Tenant Act than a guerrilla warfare manual. It dissects the act so that it is comprehensible — and, therefore, useful — to both tenants and landlords. Specifically, the book deals with all the components of the landlord-tenant relationship. Hopefully, it will answer most of the questions both landlords and tenants often ask. It explains rental agreements and shows what they should contain. It tells you what duties landlords and tenants owe to each other and explains the difference between security and damage deposits.

Other questions that are answered include: Do deposits have to be returned? Can a landlord evict a tenant by locking out the tenant or by cutting off the tenant's utility services? What is an unlawful detainer action and are there any defenses to it? Can a tenant withhold rent? How do you terminate a month-to-month rental agreement? How do you make a landlord repair the plumbing? How do you make a tenant remove the garbage? What are fair housing laws? The list goes on.

In addition to answering these questions, the book also provides practical assistance. The Landlord-Tenant Act requires both landlords and tenants to give written notices to accomplish a variety of purposes. In this book, you will find sample form notices which can be used as guides. Naturally, the forms should be used cautiously, as no form is flexible enough to cover the details of every problem.

This book is not designed to eliminate the need for lawyers. There are many problems (for example, the initiation of eviction proceedings) which require the assistance of a lawyer. You should know, however, that it is not always necessary to take legal action. Both landlords and tenants should consider arbitration as a means of settling disputes. In fact, the Landlord-Tenant Act has a series of sections which provide for the use of arbitration or mediation as means of settling disputes, which is much less expensive than court proceedings, particularly for those disputes which are relatively minor and involve small amounts of money.

At any rate, this book may serve to prevent your having to take legal measures by helping you to understand the landlord-tenant relationship better. Knowing your responsibilities, as well as your rights, beforehand, will help you to avoid many problems. Then, if worse comes to worst, you will know when to seek the assistance of a lawyer.

1
THE RESIDENTIAL
LANDLORD-TENANT ACT

Traditionally, the landlord-tenant relationship was free from government interference and could be anything the landlord or the tenant wanted. The landlord was only required to give the tenant temporary possession of the real estate and not interfere with the tenant's use of it. He did not have to make certain that the real estate was habitable or even usable. The tenant, on the other hand, had only to pay the rent and to protect the property from harm or destruction. Until 1973, this was the state of the law in Washington.

The Washington State Legislature altered the traditional landlord-tenant relationship by enacting the Residential Landlord-Tenant Act of 1973. (For convenience, in this book it will be called "the Landlord-Tenant Act" or "the act.") It changed a relationship founded upon a private agreement between the landlord and tenant to a relationship that imposes legal obligations on both parties *without regard to any agreement they might make privately.*

a. THE ACT COVERS RESIDENTIAL TENANCIES

The act does not apply to all landlord-tenant relationships — only to residential tenancies. These involve property being used by tenants as homes or as places of residence. The technical term used by the act is "dwelling unit." Therefore, a landlord-tenant relationship will be covered by the act only

1

if it involves a dwelling unit, which is defined in RCW 59.18.030* as follows:

> (1)"Dwelling unit" is a structure or that part of a structure which is used as a home, residence, or sleeping place by one person or by two or more persons maintaining a common household, including but not limited to single family residences and units of multiplexes, apartment buildings, and mobile homes.

By implication, the act would not apply to the lease of a store, an office, a warehouse, a factory, or any other real estate which is not a living arrangement. Mobile homes are covered by both this act and the provisions of the Mobile Home Landlord-Tenant Act (RCW 59.20). The Mobile Home Act relates expressly to the landlords and tenants of mobile home parks. If you occupy a mobile home in a mobile home park or are the owner of such a park, then you should consult the Mobile Home Act for a complete explanation of your rights and responsibilities.

b. NOT ALL RESIDENTIAL TENANCIES ARE COVERED

Not all landlord-tenant relationships involving dwelling units are covered by the act. Several are specifically exempted. They include the following:

(a) Educational, medical, religious, and other service-providing institutions which offer a residence to their users as part of other types of services (college dormitories, hospitals, monasteries, prisons, and recreational lodges)

The letters RCW refer to "Revised Code of Washington" which is a publication of all the current statutes enacted by the state legislature. The number "59" refers to the volume or title of that series. The number "18" refers to that chapter in title 59. The number "030" refers to that section within chapter 18 of title 59. The entire text of the Landlord-Tenant Act is contained in the Appendix.

(b) Property that is being occupied by the buyer under an earnest money agreement (a deposit) or other binding agreement to purchase that property (such as a home buyer given possession before closing date)

(c) Hotels, motels, and other businesses which primarily offer temporary housing to travelers

(d) Property being occupied by its owner after being taken by a governmental body, if the consumer protection division of the attorney general's office determines that the property is decent, safe, and sanitary

(e) Land leased for agricultural purposes; this also includes a farm house or any other building that might be used for dwelling purposes

(f) Housing that has been provided for migrant farm workers or other seasonal agricultural workers

(g) Property that is leased from the Washington Department of Natural Resources

(h) Property resided on by an employee, and that may be used only as long as the employee works for the employer-owner

(i) Single family dwellings, provided the rental agreement is for a term of more than one year and provided the tenant's attorney approves of the exemptions.

c. IT IS DIFFICULT TO AVOID BEING COVERED BY THE ACT

Unless a particular tenancy falls under one of the exceptions listed above, it is covered by the act. However, parties to a residential tenancy can agree to waive certain of the act's provisions if several procedural steps are carefully followed.

First, an agreement to waive any provision of the act cannot be contained in the rental agreement.

Second, the act prohibits a tenant from agreeing to any of the following:

(a) The tenant may not agree that if the rental agreement is broken, the landlord may get a judgment against the tenant without a court hearing.

(b) The tenant may not assume any greater obligation for the landlord's attorney's fees than that which the act provides.

(c) The tenant cannot agree to be responsible for the landlord's negligent acts.

(d) The tenant cannot agree to the appointment of a specific arbitrator at the time the tenancy begins.

(e) The tenant cannot agree that the landlord can hold the tenant's property to force the tenant to pay rent.

Third, the parties must sign a written agreement that satisfies the following requirements:

(a) The agreement may not appear in a standard or printed form lease or rental agreement; it must be written for a specific tenancy.

(b) There must be no substantial inequality in the bargaining position of the two parties. One of the parties cannot be so big and powerful that the other party is forced to sign a waiver agreement without really agreeing to it.

(c) The exemption must not violate the public policy of this state in favor of ensuring safe and sanitary housing. (The Landlord-Tenant Act is an expression of such a policy, as are local governing codes.)

(d) The local county prosecutor's office, the consumer protection division of the attorney general's office, or an attorney for the tenant must give written approval of the application for exemption, having decided that the agreement complies with the three previous requirements above.

These procedural steps make it quite difficult, if not impossible, for the parties to a residential tenancy to waive the act's coverage. Even if it is legally permissible to waive a particular provision, it would be unusual for a tenant's attorney to approve a waiver agreement. The local prosecutor or attorney general would be even more reluctant.

d. SUMMARY

The Residential Landlord-Tenant Act covers residential relationships or those that involve the use of a dwelling unit or a living arrangement. The act exempts a few special types of residential tenancies, but the act is intended to be comprehensive. Once a landlord-tenant relationship is covered, the provisions of the act can be waived only if several stringent conditions are met. In most instances, it is doubtful whether these conditions can be met.

2
STARTING A TENANCY

a. THE RENTAL AGREEMENT

Before the Landlord-Tenant Act was enacted there was a lot of confusion about the formalities to be followed before a person could legally be a landlord or a tenant. Did there have to be a written agreement? If there was a written agreement, did it have to contain certain legal language? To be valid, did an agreement have to be recorded with the county auditor? The act eliminates the confusion by allowing the parties to create a landlord-tenant relationship in almost any way they choose. The act defines a rental agreement as follows:

> "Rental agreement" means all agreements which establish or modify the terms, conditions, rules, regulations, or any other provisions concerning the use and occupancy of a dwelling unit.

A landlord-tenant relationship can be created by an oral or written agreement or both. A written agreement is required only when the parties intend to create a tenancy for a one-year term or longer. However, it is always wise to have a written agreement, because any oral agreement is effective only as long as both parties remember the terms of the agreement and only until there is a dispute. Disputes cause memories to fade and make oral agreements quite difficult to enforce.

A rental agreement needs no special language. It can be a document prepared by a lawyer, a form purchased in a stationery store, or a handwritten paper prepared by one or both of the parties. The rental agreement may consist of one document or several. Some landlords use a basic rental agreement form and attach a separate document that contains detailed rules regarding the use of the rented property. Both can be binding on the tenant. The same informality is permitted when landlords and tenants want to change their original rental agreements. It can be done in any fashion if that is what the parties intend. The importance of the rental agreement lies not in its appearance, but in whether it contains all the terms and conditions to which the parties have agreed. (Chapter 3 discusses the contents of the rental agreement.)

b. THE LANDLORD

Under the Landlord-Tenant Act you become a landlord or tenant only because the act makes you one. Both words are carefully defined by the act. As you will see, these are not dictionary definitions, but rather, they are given meanings designed to carry out the purposes of the act. The act defines "landlord" as follows:

> "Landlord" means the owner, lessor, or sublessor of the dwelling unit or the property of which it is a part, and in addition means any person designated as representative of the landlord.

Under this definition, the term "landlord" includes people who would not have been considered landlords traditionally. For example, a landlord is usually thought to be someone who has an ownership interest in property. However, by including persons who are the landlord's representatives, the act makes landlords of people employed by property owners or who perform services for property owners. Thus an apartment house manager, a person who collects rents, or even an attorney for the owner of rental property, might be called a "landlord."

The reason the act defines "landlord" so broadly is to ensure that an owner of rental property cannot avoid the obligations imposed by the act. Frequently, a tenant will not know the name or location of the property owner. Sometimes the owner does not live where the property is located. Under these circumstances, the landlord is required to designate a representative. This person will be considered a landlord. The tenant may make all complaints to this representative. The act makes giving notice to the representative the same as giving notice to the owner. The owner becomes responsible to the tenant and is required to take the corrective action required by the act once the representative receives the complaint.

c. THE TENANT

The act defines "tenant" as follows:

> A "tenant" is any person who is entitled to occupy a dwelling unit primarily for living or dwelling purposes under a rental agreement.

While the word "landlord" is given a broad definition, the word "tenant" is given a restrictive one: you are not a tenant unless you are entitled to occupy rented property. If you are a trespasser or someone occupying property without the owner's consent, then you are not a tenant.

This definition also excludes people who may be on the property with a tenant's permission but not with the consent of the landlord. An example of such a person might be a house guest or someone who is temporarily caring for the rented property in the tenant's absence.

To have the consent of the landlord, the tenant must be given permission in the rental agreement or have an express understanding with the landlord regarding the use of the property. This restrictive definition is designed to limit the landlord's responsibility to only those persons whose presence on the rented property is anticipated by the landlord.

d. TYPES OF TENANCIES

There are three common types of tenancies: month-to-month or periodic tenancies, tenancies for a specified term of less than one year, and tenancies for a term of more than one year.

The month-to-month or periodic tenancy has no termination date. It continues until one or both of the parties terminate it by written notice. It is considered a month-to-month tenancy if rent is paid on a monthly basis. It is a periodic tenancy if the rent is paid on some other regular basis.

For people who want a short-term commitment, a periodic or month-to-month tenancy is quite useful. However, the disadvantage is that it can be terminated without regard to the wishes and plans of the affected party.

The tenancy for a term of less than one year has a specific termination date and is terminated without the necessity of giving written notice. The manner in which rent is paid has no bearing on the length of this kind of tenancy. The tenancy for a term of more than one year is much the same. However, this type of tenancy differs from the other two in that it must be in writing, acknowledged, and recorded with the county auditor. These are mandatory technical requirements and if they are not followed precisely, the tenancy may not be enforceable.

If you are not sure which type of tenancy is best for you, or don't know if the tenancy gives you what you want, you should seek legal advice.

e. SUMMARY

It is relatively simple to create a landlord-tenant relationship. The parties simply enter into a rental agreement. The difficulty arises in making certain that the rental agreement contains all items agreed to by the parties. The technical requirements for a rental agreement relate primarily to a rental agreement which is to last for one year or longer. The act broadly defines "landlord" to include the landlord's designated representatives. The act narrowly defines "tenant" to exclude all persons who do not have the landlord's consent to reside in the rented property. There are three types of tenancies and the type used should depend on whether the parties want a long- or a short-term agreement.

3
THE RENTAL AGREEMENT: A SUGGESTED APPROACH

Form rental agreements can be obtained from a variety of sources, and they vary in content and purposes. Self-Counsel Press publishes a Rental Form Kit, which includes rental agreement forms and specific instructions. All preprinted forms have one characteristic in common, however: they are written in a broad, all-encompassing way so that they appear to be applicable to any situation. And that is their greatest evil. They sometimes contain language that may result in consequences that neither party intended. Therefore, forms of any kind should be used sparingly and carefully. It is always safer, and frequently cheaper in the long run, to have them reviewed and altered by someone who has some training in this area.

Sample #1 shows a rental agreement covering major points that would be found in a typical rental agreement. The commentary on the facing pages refers to the numbered paragraphs and suggests what both parties may wish to add to protect their interests. Sample #2 shows a premises checklist that should always be attached to your rental agreement.

This outline of a rental agreement contains the primary considerations landlords and tenants should have in mind when creating a landlord-tenant relationship. However, neither this outline nor the forms sold commercially ever cover all the unique problems confronting the landlord and tenant. It is always safer to consult a lawyer for assistance in the preparation and review of a rental agreement, if you have any doubts about it.

SAMPLE #1
RENTAL AGREEMENT

1. On this date <u>Tyrone Tenant and Theresa Tenant</u> (hereafter

(a)

referred to as "the Tenants") and <u>Lester Landlord</u> (hereafter

(b)

referred to as "the Landlord") entered into the following rental agreement:

2. The premises are (a single family dwelling) <u>Apt. No. 3</u> <u>in Crystal Apartments</u> located at <u>123 Rental Avenue</u>

(c)

<u>Seattle, Multnomah County, Washington.</u>
The legal description is as follows:

> Apartment 3 - 123 Rental Avenue,
> Lot 16 Plan M-79
> City of Seattle, County of Multnomah

(d)

3. The term of this agreement shall be as follows: This shall be a month-to-month tenancy and shall begin on <u>December 1, 199-</u>

4. The rent shall be <u>$400</u> per month and shall be payable in advance on or before the <u>1st</u> day of each month. The first month's rent shall be payable on <u>November 30, 199-</u>

5. The landlord and the landlord's address are as follows:

> Lester Landlord — 45678 Real Estate
> Road, Seattle
> (e)

6. There will be <u>two</u> persons occupying the premises and their names are as follows:

> Tyrone Tenant
> Theresa Tenant

COMMENTARY

1. In the first space (designated (a)) should be the names of everyone who is signing the rental agreement as tenants, including both the husband and the wife, or any individuals who will be assuming responsibility under the rental agreement.

In the second space (designated (b)) you would put the name of the owner of the building. Here you would also put the name of an agent for the owner if that person or entity has legal authority to rent the premises on behalf of the owner.

2. In line (c) you should put the street address or any other common way of describing or locating the premises.

Line (d), for the legal description, is necessary only if the rental agreement is to be recorded with the county auditor. A rental agreement needs to be recorded only if it is for a term of one year or more.

3. This section specifies how long the rental agreement is to last. The sample shows a typical periodic or month-to-month tenancy. If your agreement concerns a tenancy with a specific term, you should include both the length of the term and the date of termination. In this case, clause 3 might appear as follows:

> This shall be a 2-year tenancy and shall begin on December 1, 199- and end on November 30, 199-.

4. Rent is always payable in advance and frequently the first month's rent is paid before the tenant takes possession.

5. In line (e) you would insert the name and address of the owner of the building. As an alternative, you might insert the name and address of any person designated by the landlord as having authority to act for the landlord and the authority to accept tenants' complaints on behalf of the landlord. The act requires that either the owner or a substitute be named and that this person reside within Washington. In this case, clause 5 might read as follows:

> Artie Agent of 126 Rental Road, Seattle, is authorized to act on behalf of the landlord and is specifically authorized to accept notices of tenants' complaints and to accept any service of a Summons and Complaint as provided in RCW 59.18.060.

6. The landlord will want to know the number and identity of the people who will be occupying the premises.

Except for casual guests, no other persons shall occupy the premises without the written consent of the landlord.

7.   The landlord will provide and pay for the following utility services:

```
heating
hot and cold water
garbage removal
```

All other utility services shall be the sole responsibility of the tenant.

8.   The tenant has made an advance deposit of $100.00 of which
                                                        (f)
the landlord acknowledges receipt. This $100 will be held as a damage deposit and at the end of this tenancy all or a portion of it may be kept by the landlord to pay for actual damages caused by the tenant. Of this damage deposit, $40.00 is a nonreturnable cleaning fee and will be kept by the landlord.

The deposit will be kept at   First National Bank   which is
                                  (g)

located at   Moneyed Avenue   . At the end of the tenancy, the
              (address)

landlord will return the deposit (except a nonreturnable cleaning deposit) unless, within fourteen (14) days, the landlord gives the tenant written reasons for keeping all or a portion of it.

9.   The tenant will pay the rent as required, take good care of the premises, comply with all duties imposed by the Landlord-Tenant Act of 1973, and in particular or in addition will:

```
        keep NO pets on the premises.
```
The landlord will supply the tenant with a separate document which contains rules governing the use of the premises.

7. Utilities include heat, water, garbage, electrical, and sewer services.

8. The damage deposit, (line (f)), can only be kept if the damage is more than that caused by the ordinary wear and tear of normal use. A portion can be kept as a nonreturnable cleaning fee if the rental agreement contains an express authorization.

A security deposit might also be outlined at this point. A security deposit is to ensure that the tenant performs the obligations specified in the agreement. The deposit may be forfeited if the tenant fails to perform the obligations indicated. If no obligations are specified, the deposit must be returned. A security deposit clause might read as follows:

> This $100 will be a security deposit and all or a portion of it may be kept by the landlord if, during this tenancy, the tenant fails to do any of the following:
>
> Maintain the premises in good condition; use the plumbing and electrical appliances reasonably and safely; and keep the premises free of vermin.

In line (g) the landlord must identify the name and address of the bank or savings and loan institution in which the deposit has been placed.

9. Some rental agreements contain all the tenants' duties imposed by the Landlord-Tenant Act. Although this is not legally necessary, it does serve to remind the tenant of obligations that might otherwise be ignored or forgotten. The landlord should list any other specific concerns or refer to the existence of any separate documents which may contain rules governing the occupancy of the premises.

SAMPLE #1 — Continued

---

10. The landlord will provide the tenant with decent, safe, and sanitary premises and will comply with all duties imposed by the Landlord-Tenant Act of 1973, and in particular or in addition will:

> Provide two parking spaces
> Provide drapes and carpets
> Provide the tenant with two gallons
> of paint in colors of the tenant's
> choosing to redecorate the living room

(h)

11. Both parties have examined the premises and agree that the condition and cleanliness of and existing damages to the premises and its furnishings are accurately described in the Premises Checklist, which is attached.*

12. In addition, the parties agree as follows:

> The tenant shall not play loud music
> between the hours of 11 p.m. and 8 a.m.

13. Both parties agree that this is the entire agreement between them and that any previous oral or written agreements are no longer binding. Any modifications to this agreement will be done in writing and signed by both parties. Both parties further agree that, in any event, if a dispute between them is settled by arbitration or court proceedings, the losing party will pay the prevailing party a reasonable attorney's fee.

14. DATED: November 2, 199-

_____   _____
(Landlord)   (Tenant)

                                    _____
                                    (Tenant)

---

*See Sample #2.

COMMENTARY — Continued

10. For the same reasons given in Comment #9, the tenant may want to enumerate, in line (h), all the landlord's legal obligations. Additionally, the tenant will want to list any repairs, changes or improvements, or extras which the landlord has orally promised to make or provide.

11. This clause will help prevent later disputes over whether the present tenant or a former one caused something to be broken or damaged. A premises checklist should be attached to the agreement (see Sample #2).

12. Inevitably, the parties will have some agreement not clearly covered. It should be included here.

13. This clause tries to protect both parties against disputes involving alleged oral agreements which are not contained in the written rental agreement. It also provides incentive to comply with the agreement by making an award of attorney's fees to the party who must enforce this agreement.

14. If your rental agreement calls for a term of one year or more, it must be acknowledged by the county auditor.

A lawyer should be consulted for the proper drafting and execution of an acknowledgment as well as for the advisability of recording the rental agreement.

SAMPLE #2
PREMISES CHECKLIST

Report of rental premises and conditions on November 2, 199-. This report records the condition and contents of the rental premises located at Apartment 3, 123 Rental Avenue. If something is damaged or dirty, describe it fully on attatched sheet of paper.

	Dirty Yes*	No	Damaged Yes*	No		Dirty Yes*	No	Damaged Yes*	No
LIVING ROOM					**BATHROOM**				
Light fixture	❑	❑	❑	❑	Towel racks	❑	❑	❑	❑
Rug or carpet	❑	❑	❑	❑	Mirror	❑	❑	❑	❑
Floor	❑	❑	❑	❑	Medicine cabinet	❑	❑	❑	❑
Walls	❑	❑	❑	❑					
Ceiling	❑	❑	❑	❑	Counter top	❑	❑	❑	❑
BEDROOM					Sink	❑	❑	❑	❑
Drapes	❑	❑	❑	❑	Tub	❑	❑	❑	❑
Mirror	❑	❑	❑	❑	Shower	❑	❑	❑	❑
Light fixture	❑	❑	❑	❑	Toilet	❑	❑	❑	❑
Rug or carpet	❑	❑	❑	❑	Shower curtain	❑	❑	❑	❑
Floor	❑	❑	❑	❑	Vanity	❑	❑	❑	❑
Walls	❑	❑	❑	❑	Light fixture	❑	❑	❑	❑
Ceiling	❑	❑	❑	❑	Hot water	❑	❑	❑	❑
KITCHEN					Cold water	❑	❑	❑	❑
Cooking elements	❑	❑	❑	❑	Floor	❑	❑	❑	❑
Oven	❑	❑	❑	❑	Walls	❑	❑	❑	❑
Oven racks	❑	❑	❑	❑	Ceiling	❑	❑	❑	❑
Broiler pan	❑	❑	❑	❑	**MISCELLANEOUS**				
Refrigerator	❑	❑	❑	❑	Door key	❑	❑	❑	❑
Ice trays	❑	❑	❑	❑	Windows	❑	❑	❑	❑
Sink	❑	❑	❑	❑	Window screens	❑	❑	❑	❑
Garbage disposal	❑	❑	❑	❑	Mailbox	❑	❑	❑	❑
Counter tops	❑	❑	❑	❑	Mailbox key	❑	❑	❑	❑
Range hood	❑	❑	❑	❑	Thermostat	❑	❑	❑	❑
Dishwasher	❑	❑	❑	❑	Other*	❑	❑	❑	❑
Hot water	❑	❑	❑	❑					
Cold water	❑	❑	❑	❑					
Drawers	❑	❑	❑	❑					
Light fixture	❑	❑	❑	❑					
Floor	❑	❑	❑	❑					
Walls	❑	❑	❑	❑					
Ceiling	❑	❑	❑	❑					

*Describe fully on a separate sheet

Tenant(s)_____

Landlord (or agent)_____

Date_____

4
THE LANDLORD'S DUTIES

Duties are obligations imposed by law. The Landlord-Tenant Act imposes substantial duties upon the landlord, even if they are not expected by the tenant or mentioned in the rental agreement. This chapter and chapter 5, which deals with the duties of tenants, are two of the most important in the book. These legally imposed duties are what have so drastically changed the landlord-tenant relationship.

a. PREMISES MUST BE FIT FOR HABITATION

The landlord's duties are listed in RCW 59.18.060. There are 11 types of duties, and each will be discussed separately and interpreted in the context of the preamble of the act, which states:

> The landlord will at all times during the tenancy keep the premises fit for human habitation....

The preamble is a concise summary of all the duties owed by a landlord to a tenant. The landlord must provide a place that is habitable or one that is decent, safe, and sanitary. The phrase "fit for human habitation" is not directly defined, but given meaning from the specific duties imposed upon the landlord. Another way of looking at it is that each of the 11 types of landlord's duties are minimum standards of habitability, and if any one of them is not fulfilled, then the premises may not be fit for human habitation.

The landlord is obliged to perform all the specified duties and whatever else may be necessary to make the premises fit to reside in.

Previously, housing was considered substandard if it did not comply with any law regulating the condition of housing. For example, a housing code may have required a stair banister. If there were no banister, the premises might have been considered substandard. Now, violations of housing codes or other housing standard laws make the premises unfit for human habitation only "if such condition substantially endangers or impairs the health or safety of the tenant." Thus, violations must be quite serious before the property will be considered substandard.

However, if a landlord knowingly rents a premises which has been condemned by a government agency or is otherwise found to be uninhabitable at the time the premises are rented, the landlord can face severe penalties. These penalties include the greater of an amount equal to three months' rent or an amount equal to three times the actual damages suffered by the tenant. In the event of litigation or arbitration, the landlord may also have to pay the tenant's attorney fees.

b. COMPLIANCE WITH ALL APPLICABLE LAWS

A landlord must:

> Maintain the premises to substantially comply with any applicable code, statute, ordinance, or regulation governing their maintenance or operation, which the legislative body enacting the applicable code, statute, ordinance, or regulation could enforce as to the premises rented.

Many cities and counties have laws requiring rented property to satisfy various health and safety standards. Formerly, if the landlord failed to comply with these laws, the tenant had no right to enforce them. Now these laws are a part of the act and give the tenant power of enforcement.

For example, a city ordinance might require a landlord to provide adequate plumbing. Before the act, if the plumbing leaked, the tenant had to complain to the city's enforcing agency. That agency could decide whether or not to require the landlord to fix the plumbing. The tenant had no other way of making the landlord comply. Now, this section gives the tenant direct access to the landlord and does not limit enforcement of the ordinance to the city's enforcing agency.

c. PREMISES MUST BE STRUCTURALLY SOUND

A landlord must also:

> Maintain the roofs, floors, walls, chimneys, fireplaces, foundations, and all other structural components in reasonably good repair so as to be usable and capable of resisting any and all normal forces and loads to which they may be subjected.

These are structural requirements. The subsection does not require that the structural parts of the premises be perfect. They need only be "in reasonably good repair" to safely perform their intended functions. A foundation may be cracked as long as it adequately supports the house. A roof may have missing shingles as long as it does not leak. The structural deficiency must create or tend to create a condition which "endangers or impairs the health or safety of the tenant" before the landlord can be required to fix it.

d. COMMON AREAS MUST BE CLEAN AND SAFE

A landlord must:

> Keep any shared or common areas reasonably clean, sanitary, and safe from defects increasing the hazards of fire or accident;

A common or shared area would be most likely found in an apartment building, duplex, or other multifamily residence. It would include elevators, hallways, stairways, lobbies, and similar areas. A landlord might violate this section by failing to have adequate lighting over a stairway, by failing to have an elevator regularly inspected, or by allowing flammable materials to accumulate in a hallway.

e. INFESTATION CONTROL

A landlord must:

> Provide a reasonable program for the control of infestation by insects, rodents, and other pests at the initiation of the tenancy, and except in the case of a single family residence, control infestation during tenancy except where such infestation is caused by the tenant;

The obligation to control infestation is limited to the beginning of the tenancy and to those conditions arising during the tenancy which are not due to the tenant's fault. Thus if the tenant allows debris to collect, attracting rats and flies, it will be his or her responsibility to control them. This only applies to multifamily dwellings; single family residences are excluded.

f. REPAIRS

As a landlord, you must:

> Except where the condition is attributable to normal wear and tear, make repairs and arrangements necessary to put and keep the premises in as good condition as it by law or rental agreement should have been, at the commencement of the tenancy;

The landlord has a continuing obligation to keep the premises in good repair. However, if the condition is caused by ordinary wear and tear, then he or she is not responsible. Thus the landlord would not be responsible for painting and cleaning which is required as a result of the normal use of the premises. This subsection is really concerned with premises that are substandard or in such poor condition that they are in violation of the law at the beginning of the tenancy. In this case, the landlord must repair or improve that condition to comply with the law.

g. KEEPING THE PREMISES SECURE

A landlord must also:

> Provide reasonably adequate locks and furnish keys
> to the tenant;

The act does not define what constitutes "reasonably adequate locks." Where a local housing code exists, it may provide standards for locks. If no such standards apply, the landlord must provide a lock which is designed to keep the premises reasonably secure.

h. UTILITIES AND APPLIANCES

Furthermore, the landlord must:

> Maintain all electrical, plumbing, heating, and other
> facilities and appliances supplied by him in reason-
> ably good working order;

The landlord must provide a way for the tenant to obtain heat, water, and electricity. That does not mean that the landlord must pay for the tenant's use of these services. He or she only has to make it possible for the tenant to get these services. Furthermore, the landlord does not have an obligation to provide appliances, but if they are provided, then they must be kept in "good working order."

i. KEEPING THE PREMISES WEATHERTIGHT

The landlord must also:

> Maintain the dwelling unit in reasonably good
> weathertight condition;

Presumably this means that the roof, walls, windows, and doors should be waterproof and secure against the weather. Under some circumstances, it might even include a duty to provide insulation.

j. REMOVAL OF GARBAGE

The landlord must also:

> Except in the case of a single family residence, provide and maintain appropriate receptacles in common areas for the removal of ashes, rubbish, and garbage, incidental to the occupancy and arrange for the reasonable and regular removal of such waste;

The landlord must provide garbage cans or other facilities for collecting and disposing of refuse. This requirement does not extend to the landlord of a single family dwelling.

Landlords of duplexes and other grouped dwellings where units do not share heating and hot water equipment and where each unit has direct access to a street are excluded from this duty. Such housing is considered to be more similar to single family dwellings, which are also exempt.

k. HEAT AND WATER

The landlord must also:

> Except where the building is not equipped for the purpose, provide facilities adequate to supply heat and water and hot water as reasonably required by the tenant;

There may be some buildings in rural areas intended for use by tenants and without facilities for providing heat and water. However, most larger cities and counties would probably bar the use of such buildings as housing.

Providing means for obtaining these services is a fundamental landlord obligation. If, at the beginning of the tenancy, these facilities are not working, then the landlord must have them repaired. However, as discussed in section h, the landlord does not have to pay for the tenant's use of heat and water.

l. SMOKE DETECTOR

The landlord must also:

> Provide a written notice to the tenant that the dwelling unit is equipped with a smoke detection device as required in RCW 48.48.140. The notice shall inform the tenant of the tenant's responsibility to maintain the smoke detection device in proper operating condition and of penalties for failure to comply with the provisions of RCW 48.48.140(3). The notice must be signed by the landlord or the landlord's authorized agent and tenant with copies provided to both parties.

While landlords must install smoke detectors in their dwelling units, tenants must maintain them. By written notice, landlords must inform tenants of their obligation to replace batteries and otherwise comply with manufacturer requirements. Landlords and tenants are subject to fines of up to $200 for not fulfilling these obligations.

m. IDENTIFYING THE LANDLORD

The landlord must:

> Designate to the tenant the name and address of the person who is the landlord by a statement on the rental agreement or by a notice conspicuously posted on the premises. The tenant shall be notified immediately of any changes by certified mail or by an updated posting. If the person designated in this section does not reside in the state where the premises are located, there shall also be designated a person who resides in the county who is authorized to act as an agent for the purposes of service of notices and process, and if no designation is made of a person to act as agent, then the person to whom rental payments are to be made shall be considered such agent.

Because landlords must identify themselves, tenants now know whom to contact to make sure their landlords are fulfilling their obligations. As we will see in the next chapter, the act requires tenants to give notice if any of its provisions are violated. Landlords must either be available to receive such notices or be willing to have others receive them on their behalf.

Landlords residing outside the state must give their tenants the names and addresses of their representatives within the state. They must continually notify their tenants of all changes of address. If landlords fail to fulfill their obligations, then their rent collectors will be considered the landlords' representatives.

n. LIMITATIONS ON THE LANDLORD'S DUTIES

The purpose of the landlord's duties is to give tenants habitable premises. However, that overall purpose and the specific landlord duties are subject to two limitations.

First, if damage is caused by the tenants, their families, or their guests, landlords do not have to make repairs. Furthermore, landlords cannot be penalized for failing to make repairs if the tenants deny their landlords access to the premises.

Second, if city or county laws impose duties that cover the same areas as in subsections (2) through (11) of the act (the "duties" discussed here), but impose greater obligations, then landlords must follow the city or county laws. For example, if a local law requires a landlord to provide garbage cans for tenants of single family houses, then that requirement would supersede the lesser requirement of the act.

o. LEAD-BASED PAINT DISCLOSURES

Under federal law, a landlord must disclose the use of lead-based paint to potential tenants of housing built before 1978. This requires the landlord to provide the tenant with a lead hazard information pamphlet published by the Environmental Protection Agency. The landlord must also tell the tenant of any known use of lead-based paint and of any lead hazard evaluation report available to the landlord. The prospective tenant should be given all of this information (both verbal and written), and an opportunity to review the information, before entering into the rental agreement. Rental agreements should include a lead warning statement, a disclosure, and a tenant acknowledgment.

p. SUMMARY

A landlord must provide a tenant with premises which are fit for human habitation. The premises must be decent, safe, and sanitary. A landlord satisfies this obligation by performing all the duties enumerated in chapter 18, section 060 of the act. (See Appendix.)

5
THE TENANT'S REMEDIES

It is not much use talking about the landlord's duties to the tenant unless they can be enforced. This chapter discusses the remedies available to the tenant.

Generally, the remedy available to the tenant will depend on which duty the landlord has failed to perform and the damage or risk of damages it causes the tenant. Whatever remedy the tenant pursues, it will not be available unless the tenant has carefully satisfied several procedural steps.

Here we will also look at the controversial provision which allows the tenant to make repairs and deduct the cost from the rent. It is a very limited remedy, but it is one that allows a tenant to place economic pressure on a landlord to force the landlord to make repairs.

Finally, this chapter discusses what can be done when a tenant is threatened by other tenants or by the landlord. If the threat involves the use of firearms or the violation of a court order, the tenant may be able to vacate the premises without penalty.

a. PAYING THE RENT

Not every tenant has a legal right to complain that a landlord is not fulfilling the duties imposed by the Landlord-Tenant Act. The act provides:

> The tenant shall be current in the payment of rent before exercising any of the remedies accorded him under the provisions of this chapter: *Provided,* That this section shall not be construed as limiting the

tenant's civil remedies for negligent or intentional damages: *Provided further,* That this section shall not be construed as limiting the tenant's right in an unlawful detainer proceeding to raise the defense that there is no rent due and owing.

Ordinarily, a landlord will want to evict a tenant who owes rent and this provision gives him or her that right. Thus, a tenant cannot use the landlord's failure to perform duties as an excuse to avoid paying rent. However, in an eviction proceeding for nonpayment of rent, the tenant might have a defense controverting the landlord's claim. For example, the tenant may have performed services for the landlord in lieu of paying rent.

If a landlord initiates an eviction proceeding based on nonpayment of rent, the following provisions are applicable:

(a) The tenant must pay all rent owing and maintain current rent payments during the entire eviction proceeding, or submit a sworn statement of legal or equitable reasons about why no rent is owing.

(b) The tenant must either pay the rent into the registry of the court or provide the notice of defenses within seven days after being served with a copy of the summons and complaint.

(c) Before the landlord seeks a Writ of Restitution, the landlord must check with the court to determine whether the tenant has complied.

(d) The landlord must use a special notice provision in the unlawful detainer summons.

If the tenant does not comply with this section, then the landlord is entitled to the immediate issuance of a Writ of Restitution, which would result in a tenant eviction (see chapter 7).

This does not prevent the tenant from suing the landlord if the landlord has injured or damaged the tenant.

For example, if the landlord refused to repair faulty wiring and the wiring caused the tenant to be burned, the landlord could be sued for the injuries whether or not the rent has been paid.

This part of the act has been expanded to include "all utilities which the tenant has agreed in the rental agreement to pay." So, if the tenant agreed to pay for water, he or she must be current in rent and have paid all water bills before proceeding to make a complaint about the landlord.

b. THE TENANT MUST FIRST GIVE NOTICE

If a tenant has a complaint and is current in rent and utility payments, the tenant must first give the landlord notice of the complaint. The notice has several technical requirements:

(a) It must be in writing.

(b) It must contain the address or location of the premises.

(c) It should contain the name of the owner of the premises, if known.

(d) It should list and describe what is required of the landlord.

(e) It should be given to the landlord or someone acting for the landlord, such as the person collecting the rent.

These requirements must be closely followed. A good precautionary measure is to keep a copy of any notice that is sent or received. Sample #3 is an example of the kind of notice you would give.

c. HOW LONG DOES THE LANDLORD HAVE TO REPLY?

When the landlord receives the notice, he or she must respond. The landlord has varying time periods for making a

SAMPLE #3
NOTICE OF TENANT'S COMPLAINT

TO: Laetitia Landlady
123-559 Delapidation Boulevard

or

Clarence Caretaker
557 Delapidation Boulevard, Seattle

You rented me the premises located at Apartment #10 - 555 Delapidation Boulevard, Seattle. I took possession of these premises on or about September 1, 199- . This is a notice to you that the premises require the following repairs or conditions to be corrected:

1. The roof over the northeast bedroom is leaking. It has damaged a bed mattress and stained the bedroom floor.

2. The light over the flight of stairs connecting the 3rd and 4th floors is out and needs to be replaced.

3. A burglar broke the back door lock. The door will not lock. The lock should be replaced immediately.

4. (Describe other problems.)

Please make the requested repairs as soon as possible. You may enter the premises to make these repairs on Monday, Tuesday, or Wednesday, November 4, 5, and 6, between 9 a.m. and 4 p.m.

DATE: October 15, 199-

Apt. 10-555 Delapidation Boulevard

response, depending upon the nature of the tenant's complaint. The act provides:

> The landlord shall commence remedial action after receipt of such notice by the tenant as soon as possible but not later than the following time periods, except where circumstances are beyond the landlord's control:
>
>> (1) Not more than twenty-four hours, where the defective condition deprives the tenant of hot or cold water, heat, or electricity, or is imminently hazardous to life;
>>
>> (2) Not more than seventy-two hours, where the defective condition deprives the tenant of the use of a refrigerator, range and oven, or a major plumbing fixture supplied by the landlord; and
>>
>> (3) Not more than ten days in all other cases.

In each instance the burden shall be on the landlord to see that remedial work under this section is completed promptly. If completion is delayed due to circumstances beyond the landlord's control, including the unavailability of financing, the landlord shall remedy the defective condition as soon as possible.

Note that the landlord is required only to "commence" and not necessarily "complete" the required repairs. It is also significant that the landlord may not be penalized for delay if the delay is caused by "circumstances...beyond the landlord's control." This would include any time that the tenant unreasonably denied the landlord access to the premises.

The first two sections are very clear in their time requirements, with Section (3) applying to all other kinds of repairs. The last paragraph recognizes that the landlord's inability to finance the repairs may permit some delay. However, the landlord must still proceed "promptly," and it will be up to the landlord to prove that any delay in making repairs is legally justified.

d. SUPPOSE THE LANDLORD DOES NOT RESPOND?

If, after the time periods we have just discussed have expired, the landlord fails to respond, the tenant has three remedies: the tenant may terminate the rental agreement; he or she may initiate arbitration or litigation proceedings; or the tenant may make repairs and deduct their cost from the rent.

1. Terminate the rental agreement

To terminate the rental agreement, the tenant must give the landlord a written notice. The notice must give the reasons for termination and the date on which the tenant intends to leave (see Sample #4). On the termination date, the tenant shall have no further obligation to pay rent and will be entitled to a pro rata (proportionate) return of any prepaid rent. The tenant may also recover all or a portion of a prepaid damage deposit.

2. Lawsuits and arbitration proceedings

The tenant may file a lawsuit, or, if the landlord agrees, the tenant's claim can be determined by arbitration. If the judge or the arbitrator determines that the landlord has not complied with the act, then the following relief can be provided.

(a) The landlord can be ordered to make the required repairs, or the tenant can be authorized to make them at the expense of the landlord.

(b) The rent can be reduced if it is determined that the defective condition has reduced the rental value of the premises. For example, if a leaky roof prevents the use of one bedroom in a three-bedroom house, the rent might be reduced by one-third. The reduced rent can be made retroactive to the date the tenant first gave written notice of the defective condition and can be made to continue until the defective condition has been repaired.

SAMPLE #4
NOTICE OF TERMINATION OF TENANCY
FOR LANDLORD'S FAILURE TO
RESPOND TO COMPLAINTS

TO: Lester Landlord
45678 Real Estate Road

or

Artie Agent
Apt. 1 - 123 Rental Avenue

On May 1, 199- , you were notified that the premises I rent from you at Apt. No. 10 - 678 Rotten Row required certain repairs to be made or conditions to be corrected. As of this time, you have not done as requested in the following respects:

1. No heating

2. Roof leaks

3. Front lock does not work

Because you have not done as I have requested, you are notifed that our rental agreement is terminated. I will vacate the premises on June 15, 199- .

DATE: May 30, 199-

Apt. No. 10 - 678 Rotten Row

(c) The rental agreement can be terminated if it is determined that the defective condition is so serious that it could not be repaired within the time limits allowed by the act, and it makes the premises so dangerous that the tenant should vacate. The tenant will be given a reasonable period of time to vacate.

3. Right to withhold rent and make repairs for nondangerous conditions

Under some circumstances, a tenant may repair or arrange to have others repair the defective condition. This is one of the most technical provisions of the act. It is a self-help measure that allows a tenant to make limited repairs and deduct the cost of these repairs from the rent payment. Both the type of repair and its cost are limited. It may not be used to force compliance with two types of landlord duties — the duty to provide garbage cans, and the duty of a landlord to designate a representative. If this provision is used to make the landlord provide adequate locks, the tenant must provide the landlord with a key to any new lock installed.

There are two types of self-help repair remedies. One is commonly known as "estimate and repair" and the other is known as "repair and deduct." Estimate and repair is used for more serious and costlier types of repairs. Repair and deduct is used for minor repairs, which can usually be done by the tenant.

(a) Repairs by someone other than the tenant (estimate and repair)

If the landlord has received written notice of the defect and has not reasonably responded, the tenant can hire others to make the repairs only if the following steps are taken. The tenant must get a repair cost estimate from a licensed or registered person who is competent to make the repairs. The estimate must be given to the landlord and can be given at the same time the tenant gives notice of a complaint. It is not necessary for the tenant to get more than one estimate or to get a formal bid. The landlord is given an opportunity to evaluate the estimate. If, after receiving the estimate, the landlord does not make the repairs within the time period allowed by the act, the tenant may have the repairs made by the person who provided the estimate.

If the condition to be repaired is one for which the landlord has 10 days to repair, then the tenant must wait at least 10 days after notice is given or at least 5 days after the landlord receives notice of the tenant's intention to make repairs before authorizing the work to proceed. After the work is completed, the landlord has a right to inspect it. When these steps have been completed, the tenant can deduct the cost of the repairs from a monthly rental payment, even if the actual repair costs exceed the estimate, but total repair costs cannot exceed one month's rent. This remedy can be used more than once during a 12-month period, but the total deducted cannot exceed the equivalent of two month's rent.

To illustrate, assume that the monthly rent is $300 and in one month a water line breaks at a repair cost of $100. In another month, the refrigerator gives out, costing $200.

A reasonable time for response would be 24 hours in the case of the water line and 72 hours in the case of the refrigerator. If the tenant has obtained the required estimates and the landlord has not made the repairs within those time periods, then the tenant can have the repairs made. The cost of both repairs could be deducted, as each does not total more than one month's rent.

In a third month, the roof starts leaking at an estimated repair cost of $800. The landlord has 10 days within which to begin making the repairs, but has only 5 days after receiving the repair estimate to decide whether or not to let the tenant make the repairs. If the tenant gave the landlord the repair estimate and the notice of the leak in the roof at the same time, then the landlord would have 10 days to begin the repair work. However, the roof repair cannot be made under the self-help provision. Its $800 cost exceeds twice the amount of the monthly rent within a 12-month period. Had the repair cost been $300 or less, then the repair and deduction could be made. The tenant must use one of the other remedies.

(b) Repairs by the tenant (repair and deduct)

The second type of self-help remedy is even more limited. It authorizes the tenant to make the repairs personally if the cost does not exceed one month's rent and if total repair costs for any 12-month period do not exceed one month's rent. The repairs must not be the kind that would ordinarily be made by a licensed or registered craftsperson. The repairs must be made in a competent manner and must conform to all applicable housing and building codes.

If these conditions are met and the landlord has inspected the repair work, the tenant may deduct the repair cost from one month's rent.

(c) Agreement to make repairs and repair work poorly done

Neither of the self-help remedies prevents the landlord and tenant from agreeing that the tenant can make repairs for a rent reduction or cash payment. Their agreement would not be subject to any of the limitations placed on the self-help remedies, but would have to comply with other applicable provisions of the Landlord-Tenant Act. Furthermore, the self-help provisions do not require the landlord to accept repair work which is poorly done. The tenant is responsible for any work done under these provisions and must compensate the landlord for any damages he or she may cause.

4. Right to withhold rent and make repairs for dangerous conditions

Under some circumstances repair needs may be so serious as to "substantially endanger or impair the safety of the tenant."

These include —

(i) structural members that are of insufficient size or strength to carry imposed loads with safety,

(ii) exposure of the occupants to the weather,

(iii) plumbing and sanitation defects that directly expose the occupants to the risk of illness or injury,

(iv) lack of water, including hot water,

(v) heating or ventilation systems that are not functional or are hazardous,

(vi) defective, hazardous, or missing electrical wiring or electrical services, or

(vii) conditions that increase the risk of fire.

As with other repair needs, the tenant must notify the landlord and give the landlord an opportunity to make the repairs. If the landlord does not respond, the tenant may ask a local government housing agency to inspect the premises. An inspection should take place within five days. The landlord has a right to be present during the inspection. If the inspection confirms the tenant's claims that the conditions are a threat to the tenant's health and safety, the inspector shall provide the tenant with written certification.

At this point the tenant must determine whether the repairs can be made under the self-help provisions of the Landlord-Tenant Act. If not, the tenant then has the option of setting up an escrow account and paying rent into this account rather than to the landlord.

Setting up an escrow account is not an easy process and legal assistance is advised. First, an escrow company must be selected. This can be a bank or other financial institution, an attorney, or any business authorized to act as an escrow agent. Next, the tenant must provide the landlord with a copy of the local government certification that the premises are dangerous and, along with it, a sworn written notice of the tenant's intention to create an escrow account. The written notice must be in the form shown in Sample #5.

The notice may be either mailed by first class mail or delivered to the landlord personally. In either case the notice must be given to the landlord within 24 hours after the tenant deposits the rent payment in escrow.

Upon receipt of the notice of escrow, the landlord can get the money released by providing certification from the local government housing agency that the repairs have been satisfactorily completed. The landlord also has the option of filing a lawsuit to contest the validity of the escrow account. In this lawsuit, the landlord may also ask the court to release the withheld rent in order to pay "the debt service on the premises, the insurance premiums for the premises, utility services, and repairs to the rental unit."

The tenant must be informed and may countersue the landlord for the extent to which the needed repairs have caused the premises to be reduced in value. However, as long as the tenant pays the full amount of the rent owed into the escrow account when it is due, the landlord may not evict the tenant for nonpayment of rent. The winning party in such a lawsuit is entitled to have his or her attorney fees paid.

5. Be very careful about withholding rent

A word of caution is necessary. A limited right to withhold rent exists to make self-help repairs and a more extended right of withholding exists when the condition of the premises creates a threat to human safety. However, these procedures are complex and if not followed to the letter, the tenant may be evicted. Because the risks are so great, legal advice should always be obtained.

SAMPLE #5
NOTICE TO LANDLORD OF RENT ESCROW

Name of tenant: Tilly Tenant

Name of landlord: Lofty Landlord

Name and address of escrow:

Escrow Company
1700 Busy Street
Sometown, WA 11111

Date of deposit of rent into escrow: January 6, 199-

Amount of rent deposited into escrow: $600

The following condition has been certified by a local building official to substantially endanger, impair, or affect the health or safety of a tenant: The water line into the premises has broken and I have no water.

That written notice of the conditions needing repair was provided to the landlord on January 2, 199-, and 24 hours have elapsed and the repairs have not been made.

_____

Subscribed and sworn to before me, a Notary Public residing in the City of _____Seattle_____, State of Washington

_____

My commission expires June 10, 199-

e. WHAT IF I AM THREATENED WITH VIOLENCE?

Obviously, if a tenant is threatened with violence, the police should be notified promptly. However, the tenant also has a right to expect the landlord to provide the tenant with safe premises. This means that the landlord must not harm the tenant and also means that the landlord must protect the tenant from other tenants who threaten acts of violence.

If the landlord breaches this duty, the tenant may be able to terminate the tenancy, if the following conditions are satisfied:

> If a tenant notifies the landlord that he or she, or another tenant who shares that particular dwelling unit has been threatened by another tenant, and:
>
> > (1) The threat was made with a firearm or other deadly weapon … and
> >
> > (2) The tenant who made the threat is arrested as a result of the threatening behavior; and
> >
> > (3) The landlord fails to file an unlawful detainer action against the tenant who threatened another tenant within seven calendar days after receiving notice of the arrest from a law enforcement agency; then the tenant who was threatened may terminate the rental agreement and quit the premises upon written notice to the landlord without further obligation under the rental agreement.

The landlord must then make a "a pro rata refund of any prepaid rent" and refund any prepaid deposit unless the landlord provides the tenant with written reasons for withholding the deposit.

The same remedy is available to the tenant if it is the landlord who is threatening the tenant and if the landlord is arrested for that reason. Here the rental agreement and the duty to pay rent are ended at the date of the landlord's arrest.

41

A similar remedy arises when the tenant has a protective court order that is violated. Again several conditions must be met.

> If a tenant notifies the landlord in writing that:
>
> > (1) He or she has a valid order for protection; and
> >
> > (2) The person to be restrained has violated the order since the tenant occupied the dwelling unit; and
> >
> > (3) The tenant has notified the sheriff of the county or the peace officers of the municipality in which the tenant resides of the violation; and
> >
> > (4) A copy of the order for protection is available for the landlord.

Once the tenant gives the landlord this notice the obligation to pay rent ends and the tenant is entitled to pro rata payment of any prepaid rent and also any deposit, if not contested in writing by the landlord.

f. RENTING A CONDEMNED PREMISES

Should the landlord rent the tenant premises that a government agency has condemned or otherwise declared to be unfit for housing, the tenant has significant remedies. If the enforcing agency does not force the tenant to move and the tenant elects to remain in the housing, the landlord may be forced to pay the tenant treble damages. If the tenant terminates the tenancy, the tenant may also recover all deposits paid the landlord.

g. RENTING A PREMISES THAT SUBSTANTIALLY IMPAIRS A TENANT'S HEALTH AND SAFETY

A tenant may not discover that a premises has serious repair needs until residing in it for a period of time. If these repair needs are so serious as to "endanger or impair the health of the tenant," the tenant may follow a procedure which ultimately permits payment of the rent into an escrow account.

However, the tenant must follow several steps including initiation of a complaint with a local government housing enforcement agency.

As with all other repair needs, the tenant must first give written notice to the landlord. If the landlord does not respond within the time permitted, the tenant may ask for an inspection by an enforcement agency of a local government. The government inspection will verify the accuracy of the tenant's claims and certify whether or not the repair needs make the premises a substantial risk to the health and safety of the tenant. A written report will be provided to the landlord and tenant.

If the report supports the tenant's claims, the tenant must then determine whether the repairs can be made and paid for as deductions from rent payment. If the repair costs exceed the "repair and deduct" limitations, the tenant may then elect to pay rent into an approved escrow account. If the tenant takes this step, the tenant must provide the landlord with a sworn written notice of intent to pay rent into escrow. The notice must contain: the name and address of the escrow account, the amount of rent to be paid into escrow, a description of the conditions found to be a threat to health and safety, the date the landlord was first notified, and the time elapsed with no repairs being made.

The landlord must file a court action to get the return of the rent held in escrow. The tenant is a party to that action and the court can determine how the rent is to be paid. The landlord may get the rent returned, but may also have to pay the tenant for escrow costs and legal costs, and make up for rent charged in excess of the diminished value of the premises. If the tenant fails to make regular rent payments into the escrow account, the tenant may be evicted for nonpayment of rent.

This procedure is quite complex and if not followed as required, the tenant may be worse off than if some other remedy was followed. Legal advice should be sought before attempting any kind of rent withholding.

h. SUMMARY

A tenant has several methods of enforcing a landlord's duties. Before any enforcement remedy is available, the tenant must give written notice of the complaint and give the landlord an opportunity to respond. The time given the landlord for a response depends upon the type of repair required and varies from less than 24 hours to no more than 10 days. If the landlord fails to comply, the tenant has these options:

(a) Terminate the rental agreement

(b) Bring a lawsuit or an arbitration proceeding to have the repairs made or obtain a reduction in the rent

(c) Use a self-help remedy by having someone other than the landlord make the repairs and deduct their cost from a rent payment

(d) If living in condemned housing, a claim may be made for treble damages along with the return of any deposits made

(e) Pay the rent into a rent escrow account if the landlord fails to repair a condition that is a threat to the tenant's safety

The last two options are quite restrictive and must be exercised with caution. The tenant also has important remedies if threatened with violence or if protected by a court order. If a tenant threatens violence and is arrested by the police and the landlord takes no action, the tenant victim may terminate the tenancy. If a landlord threatens the tenant and is arrested, the tenant victim may terminate the tenancy. If a tenant has a protective court order, which is violated by another tenant and which is known to the landlord and local police, the tenant victim may terminate the tenancy.

6
THE TENANT'S DUTIES

The Landlord-Tenant Act is not one-sided. Tenants, like land-lords, also have duties imposed on them. To some extent the duties imposed on a tenant do not have as much of an effect on the traditional landlord-tenant relationship as do those imposed on the landlord. The tenant has always been re-quired to take reasonably good care of the landlord's prop-erty. Also, the relatively unequal bargaining power between a landlord and tenant permits the landlord to impose greater duties on the tenant than the tenant can impose on the landlord ("if you refuse to agree to my terms, then you cannot rent my property").

a. PAYING RENT AND COMPLYING WITH THE LAWS

Tenant's duties are discussed in RCW 59.18.130, where they are arranged in six subsections. The section starts with the following requirement:

> Each tenant shall pay the rental amount at such times and in such amounts as provided for in the rental agreement or as otherwise provided by law and com-ply with all obligations imposed upon tenants by applicable provisions of all municipal, county, and state codes, statutes, ordinances, and regulations...

The tenant's fundamental obligation is to pay rent. That obligation exists even if not contained in a rental agreement. If no specific rent payment is agreed upon, then the tenant must pay a reasonable amount of rent. In any dispute over whether rent has been paid, the tenant has the burden of proving payment. Without documentation of payment, like a cancelled check, a tenant may not be able to prove payment. A tenant should always demand a receipt for a rent payment that is not made by check. Upon demand, the landlord must provide a receipt for all payments made.

The tenant must also comply with all applicable city and county laws. This obligation is similar to that placed on the landlord. Local laws must be complied with even though they are not in the rental agreement. For example, if a city ordinance requires a tenant to keep sidewalks free from snow, the tenant must comply even if the landlord does not care whether or not the snow is removed.

The landlord may not keep the tenant's personal property as a means of receiving payment of rent or performance of other obligations. That section of the act is clarified by requiring the tenant to make a written demand that the landlord return the tenant's property. If, thereafter, the landlord still refuses to return the property, the tenant may file a lawsuit.

b. KEEPING THE PREMISES CLEAN

According to subsection (1), the tenant must:

> Keep that part of the premises which he occupies and uses as clean and sanitary as the conditions of the premises permit;

Traditionally, the tenant had a duty not to intentionally damage the landlord's property or act in a negligent manner which would result in damage. However, the tenant did not have to keep the landlord's property clean and sanitary. Subsection (1) adds this responsibility. However, the act does not state what constitutes a clean and sanitary condition, and reasonable people could certainly disagree as to whether or not the premises are clean. Some limitation is provided by making the condition vary, depending on the nature of the premises involved. The standards for determining a clean and sanitary condition in an old dilapidated building will be much lower than for a newer, well-kept building.

c. REMOVING GARBAGE AND FUMIGATING

According to subsection (2), the tenant must:

> Properly dispose from his dwelling unit all rubbish, garbage and other organic or flammable waste, in a clean and sanitary manner at reasonable and regular intervals and assume all costs of extermination and fumigation for infestation caused by the tenant;

This expands and provides some detail to subsection (1). One person's garbage may be another's work of art, but this section requires it to be removed if it is unsanitary or flammable. The section also limits the landlord's duty to keep the premises free of infestation by shifting the duty to the tenant when the tenant creates the condition.

d. USING UTILITY FIXTURES AND APPLIANCES PROPERLY

Under subsection (3), the tenant must:

> Properly use and operate all electrical, gas, heating, plumbing and other fixtures and appliances supplied by the landlord;

A landlord will often supply a washer and dryer or other appliances. The tenant must use these appliances in a responsible manner or pay for any damages caused or repairs required. The same obligation exists for all utility fixtures.

e. A TENANT MUST NOT HARM THE PREMISES

Under subsection (4), the tenant must:

> Not intentionally or negligently destroy, deface, impair, or remove any part of the structure or dwelling with the appurtenances thereto, including the facilities, equipment, furniture, furnishings, and appliances, or permit any member of his family, invitee,

licensee, or any person acting under his control to do so;

This is a traditional tenant duty. The tenant has a right to use, but not abuse, rented premises. The liability of the tenant extends to any harm which is caused through the fault of the tenant and which is not due to ordinary wear and tear. The liability extends not only to the tenant and the tenant's family, but includes anyone on the premises with the tenant's consent. For example, if a visitor's child throws a rock through a window, the tenant is responsible for its repair.

Finally, if the tenant intentionally destroys the landlord's property, a tenant may be subject to criminal prosecution.

f. A TENANT MUST NOT USE THE PREMISES FOR AN IMPROPER PURPOSE

Under subsection (5), a tenant must:

Not permit a nuisance or common waste;

"Nuisance" and "waste" are legal terms. Both relate to using the landlord's property in an illegal manner or in a way that is destructive to the property. For example, if the premises are used for gambling purposes in violation of state law, that would be considered a nuisance. A waste of the premises would occur if it is used for any unintended purpose, such as using a residence as an animal shelter.

g. A TENANT MAY NOT ENGAGE IN UNLAWFUL DRUG ACTIVITY

Under subsection (6), a tenant must:

Not engage in drug-related activity at the rental premises, or allow a subtenant, sublessee, resident, or anyone else to engage in drug-related activity at the rental premises with the knowledge or consent of the tenant. "Drug-related activity" means that activity which constitutes a violation of chapter 69.41, 69.50, or 69.52 RCW;

48

Little explanation is required here. Unlawful drug use of any kind is prohibited. The prohibition is broad enough to include guests of the tenant.

h. MAINTAIN SMOKE DETECTOR IN WORKING CONDITION

Under subsection (7), a tenant must:

> Maintain the smoke detection device in accordance with the manufacturer's recommendations, including the replacement of batteries where required for the proper operation of the smoke detection device...

The landlord must provide a smoke detector in each dwelling unit, but the tenant must keep it working. Normally, this means just keeping fresh batteries in the detector, although if it does not work for some other reason, the tenant must promptly notify the landlord. Under a separate statute the landlord and the tenant can be subject to a fine of up to two hundred dollars for not fulfilling their respective duties.

i. DO NOT THREATEN OR ASSAULT THE LANDLORD OR OTHER TENANTS

Under subsection (8), a tenant must:

> Not engage in any activity at the rental premises that is:
>
> > (a) Imminently hazardous to the physical safety of other persons on the premises; and
> >
> > (b)(i) Entails physical assaults upon another person which result in an arrest; or
> >
> > (ii) Entails the unlawful use of a firearm or other deadly weapon ... which results in an arrest, including threatening another tenant or the landlord with a firearm or other deadly weapon...

The tenant is not to be a personal threat to tenants or to the landlord. Such a tenant will not only be evicted, but quite likely will face criminal prosecution. In addition, the law provides special protection to the tenant who is the victim.

While the landlord may evict the tenant who is causing the trouble, the landlord may not evict the tenant who is the victim.

j. AVOID GANG-RELATED ACTIVITY

Under subsection (9), an tenant must:

> Not engage in any gang-related activity at the premises...or allow another to engage in such activity at the premises, that renders people in at least two or more dwelling units or residences insecure in life or the use of property or that injures or endangers the safety or health of people in at least two or more dwelling units or residences.

Whether an activity constitutes gang-activity for which the tenant is responsible depends on a number of factors. The number of individuals involved, the number and nature of complaints made, damage to property, harassment of other tenants, and police involvement will be considered. For tenant responsibility, the tenant must be directly involved with a gang or have the ability to limit gang activities.

k. RETURNING THE PREMISES IN GOOD CONDITION

Under subsection (10), a tenant must:

> Upon termination and vacation, restore the premises to their initial condition except for reasonable wear and tear or conditions caused by failure of the landlord to comply with his obligations under this chapter: *Provided,* That the tenant shall not be charged for normal cleaning if he has paid a nonrefundable cleaning fee.

The obligation to return the premises in the same condition as first rented (allowing for the deterioration caused by ordinary use) is another traditional tenant obligation. Difficulties arise when either or both of the parties forget or have no records showing the original condition of the premises.

Therefore, the landlord and the tenant are well advised to both agree on the condition in which they found the premises at the beginning of the tenancy — in writing.

Common disputes involve holes in the carpet, cracked window panes, and damaged appliances. Written verification of such problems will avoid dispute when the tenancy is completed. The Self-Counsel *Rental Form Kit* includes a form to record the condition of the premises and contents.

A more difficult problem concerns the question of whether or not changes in the premises are the kind that the landlord should have expected as ordinary wear and tear. If they are, then the tenant has no responsibility for them. (This will be discussed further in chapter 8, which deals with damage deposits.)

Returning the premises in the same condition means they should be as clean as when the tenant obtained possession. However, as the last part of the section indicates, the landlord can waive this requirement by accepting a nonrefundable cleaning deposit. This means that the landlord intends to do all the required cleaning.

l. DUTIES IMPOSED BY THE LANDLORD

The duties just discussed are imposed on the tenant whether or not they are contained in the rental agreement. The landlord may raise the rent or require the tenant to comply with additional rules regarding the use, care, and maintenance of the premises. These rules must be reasonable and must not be contrary to the duties imposed upon the landlord. Examples include rules concerning pets, the use of communal washers and dryers, parking privileges, guests, and similar matters.

The landlord only has to notify the tenant of these rules at the beginning of the tenancy and provide the tenant with a copy of them. The landlord can raise the rent or change these rules by giving the tenant written notice of changes at least 30 days before the end of a tenancy.

This means that in a month-to-month tenancy, notice would have to be given at least 30 days before the beginning of the next month. If the notice is late, the effect of the rule will be delayed one month.

m. SUMMARY

A tenant must pay rent and protect the landlord's property from any harm and any unexpected damage. A tenant has the duty to keep the premises clean and sanitary. A landlord can also impose other duties on the tenant. To be binding these rules must be disclosed to the tenant when the tenancy begins. They can be changed by giving the tenant adequate notice.

7
THE LANDLORD'S REMEDIES

If a tenant does not perform the duties described in chapter 6, generally, the landlord can either force the tenant to perform them or terminate the tenancy, evicting the tenant.

a. THE LANDLORD MUST GIVE NOTICE

As with tenants, a landlord has no remedy unless certain preliminary steps are taken first. If the landlord has a complaint, he or she must first notify the tenant. Failure to provide proper notification may be interpreted as meaning that the landlord does not want the tenant to fulfill his or her legal obligations. Notice requirements include all the following:

(a) The notice must be in writing.

(b) The notice must be directed to the tenant and contain an accurate description of the landlord's complaint, stating what action the tenant is required to take.

(c) It must be given to the tenant within a reasonable time after the landlord has learned of the deficiency.

(d) The notice will be effective for 60 days after it has been given to the tenant.

Sample #6 is an example of a notice a landlord should use.

However, this kind of notice is not required when:

(a) a tenant is accused of engaging in a drug related activity, or

(b) a tenant is arrested for threatening or assaulting other tenants or the landlord.

SAMPLE #6
NOTICE OF LANDLORD'S COMPLAINT

TO: Sam Sot-Weed (Tenant)
10 Renters' Avenue
Seattle, Washington

You occupy the premises located at 10 Renters' Avenue. You took possession of these premises on or about April 1, 199- .

This is notice to you that the premises require the following repairs or conditions to be corrected:

1. You have allowed garbage to accumulate on the front doorstep. It should be removed.

2. You are keeping a horse in the back yard in violation of a city ordinance. Remove the horse at once.

Please make these repairs or correct these conditions as soon as possible.

DATE: July 1, 199-

2 Mungummory Street,
Seattle, Washington

In both instances, the landlord need not give prior notice, but may proceed directly to evict the tenant.

b. HOW SOON MUST THE TENANT REPLY?

After receiving notice, the tenant must respond within a reasonable period of time. Unlike the landlord, the tenant must not just *begin* the requested action, but must actually *complete* it within the allotted time. Whether or not the time taken by the tenant is reasonable depends on the nature of the condition to be corrected. The tenant has 30 days to correct a condition that —

(a) can substantially affect the health and safety of the tenant or other tenants, or

(b) substantially increase the hazards of fire or accident that can be remedied by repair, replacement of a damaged item, or cleaning.

If whatever the tenant has done or is allowing to occur is so serious as to create an emergency condition, then the tenant must correct it "as promptly as conditions require." Obviously, this means a time period which is less than 30 days.

There will be differences of opinion as to whether or not a condition to be corrected creates an emergency or not. The landlord is entitled to make that initial determination and to set the time for corrective action. In making this determination, the landlord must act reasonably. Thereafter, the tenant must comply. If the tenant believes that the landlord has acted unreasonably, this may be a good defense to any legal action by the landlord.

By way of illustration, assume that a tenant allowed garbage to accumulate, attracting flies and rats. The tenant resided in a single family dwelling and only the tenant was affected. It would be reasonable for the landlord to give the tenant 30 days to remove the garbage. The garbage could be a substantial threat, but it does not create an emergency.

Assume that a tenant unlawfully and improperly rewired a room to conduct dangerous electrical experiments. Suppose also that the tenant resided in an apartment building. This could be considered an emergency, for there may be an immediate fire hazard which could jeopardize the lives of all the tenants. Corrective action should be made immediately. Additionally, the wiring should be done by licensed personnel and the tenant would have to pay this expense.

c. SUPPOSE THE TENANT DOES NOT RESPOND?

If the tenant does not respond as requested, the landlord has three remedies. The landlord can —

(a) make the repairs at the expense of the tenant,

(b) initiate legal action to compel performance or collect damages, or

(c) evict the tenant.

1. Make repairs at the tenant's expense

A landlord choosing to correct the conditions may enter the tenant's premises for that purpose. However, except in the case of an emergency, the landlord should not enter without first getting the tenant's consent or without first giving the tenant two days' notice of the intent to enter. Entry should be made during the daytime or at a time convenient to the tenant.

After entering and correcting the condition, the landlord can bill the tenant for the actual cost of the work done. Unless other arrangements are made, the tenant must pay the bill no later than the date set for the next rent payment. If the tenancy has been terminated, the bill is payable immediately.

2. Lawsuits and arbitration proceedings

A landlord may prefer to seek the assistance of an arbitrator, who may either direct the tenant to take the corrective action requested by the landlord or give the tenant the option of doing the requested work or vacating.

On the other hand, the landlord may get a judgment for the damages caused by the tenant, and it can be collected through attachment, garnishment, or other collection proceedings. The implementation of this remedy usually requires the services of a lawyer.

3. Eviction proceedings — the unlawful detainer action

Finally, a landlord may decide to terminate the tenancy. Formerly, some landlords resorted to a variety of informal methods to encourage the tenant to leave. One method was to lock the tenant out of the premises. Another was to shut off the utilities.

The Landlord-Tenant Act prohibits both these remedies. If a landlord locks out a tenant, the tenant will be entitled to a court order either restoring possession or terminating the tenancy. The tenant will also be awarded any damages suffered as a result of the lockout; the landlord will also have to pay court costs and the tenant's attorney's fees. *So remember, lockouts and utility shut-offs are unlawful.*

The unlawful detainer action is the only way one can evict a tenant who is unwilling to vacate voluntarily. This is a very complex lawsuit with numerous procedural requirements and pitfalls. Therefore, the unlawful detainer action should neither be initiated nor defended without the assistance of an attorney.

What follows is an outline of what the lawsuit involves and particular considerations such as required notices, defenses and bonds.

(a) Notice requirements

An unlawful detainer action cannot be started until the tenant has been given notice. There are two types of notices. One terminates the tenancy by giving the tenant a specific termination date. This notice could be used to terminate a month-to-month tenancy by giving the tenant 20 or more days' notice of the tenancy end.

The second type of notice gives the tenant a period of time to either comply with a particular demand or face termination of the tenancy. This notice could be used to force the payment of delinquent rent by giving the tenant three days to either pay rent or vacate the premises. A special variation of this second type of notice applies to premises located within the City of Seattle. The City of Seattle requires evictions to be based on cause. An eviction notice to tenants within the City of Seattle must state the reasons for the eviction and give the tenant an opportunity to correct the claimed problems.

Here is a summary of the more common notice requirements:

(a) The notice must be in writing.

(b) If the landlord is evicting the tenant for not paying rent, the notice must state the amount of rent owing and must give the tenant three days to either pay the rent or vacate the premises. The notice will be improper if it does not give the tenant the alternative of either paying or vacating (see Sample #7).

(c) If the landlord is evicting the tenant because he or she has not complied with the provisions of the rental agreement or has not fulfilled those duties described in chapter 6, the notice must state exactly what the tenant has not done. It must give the tenant the alternative of either correcting the deficiency within 10 days or vacating the premises (see Sample #8).

SAMPLE #7
THREE-DAY NOTICE TO PAY RENT OR VACATE

TO: Lara Lastflinger (tenant)
123 Penniless Lane

You occupy the premises located at Apartment 10, 123 Penniless Lane, Washington under a rental agreement requiring you to pay monthly rent of $250. This is notice to you that you have not paid rent for the months of April, May and June and you now owe $750.

You are given three (3) days after being served with this notice to either pay the rent, amounting to $750 or, as an alternative, to vacate the premises.

If you fail to comply with this notice, unlawful detainer proceedings may be initiated against you.

DATED: June 30, 199-

Apartment 2, 123 Penniless Lane
Washington

SAMPLE #8
TEN-DAY NOTICE TO CORRECT DEFICIENCIES
OR VACATE

TO: Sam Sot-Weed (tenant)
     10 Renters' Avenue, Seattle

You occupy the premises located at 10 Renters' Avenue, Washington. You took possession of these premises on or about April 1, 199-. This is notice to you that the premises require the following repairs or conditions to be corrected:

1.   You have allowed garbage to accumulate on the front door step. It must be removed.

2.   You are keeping a horse in the back yard in violation of a city ordinance. Remove the horse at once.

You are given 10 (ten) days after the service of this notice upon you to either do as requested above or vacate the premises.

If you fail to comply with this notice, unlawful detainer proceedings may be initiated against you.

DATE: July 30, 199-

2 Mungummory Street, Seattle

(d) If the tenant is being evicted for engaging in drug activities, gang-related activities, or other unlawful activities, or activities that are a threat to persons or property, the notice must give the tenant three days to vacate. This notice does not have to give the tenant any alternative (see Sample #9).

(e) If the basis of the eviction is the termination of a month-to-month or other periodic tenancy, the notice must notify the tenant of the date of termination. Except as noted in (f), no reasons need to be given. The notice must be given to the tenant more than 20 days before the date on which rent is normally paid (see Sample #10).

(f) If the premises are located in the City of Seattle, the city's Just Cause Ordinance must be consulted. This ordinance requires written reasons for every eviction. Its effect is to preclude use of the 20-day notice described in (e).

In all cases, the notice must be delivered to the tenant. If the tenant is unavailable or is avoiding service of the notice, the notice may be posted on the door of the premises and a copy mailed to the tenant by certified mail, return receipt requested.

The landlord or any of the landlord's agents may serve the notice. The notice may be served on the tenant or any member of the tenant's family if the individual served is old enough to understand that notice is to be given to an adult.

Careful records must be kept of the day and the time of the day that the notice is served. Frequently, the person serving the notice must sign an affidavit containing the time, place, name of individual served, and method of service.

(b) Summons and complaint

Assuming a proper notice has been served, the next step is to prepare and serve a summons and complaint. The summons

SAMPLE #9
THREE-DAY NOTICE TO VACATE
(Illegal or harmful activities)

TO: Sam and Sadie Slick (tenants)
Apartment 3, Roulette Row, Anycity

You occupy the premises located at Apartment 3, Roulette Row, Anycity. You took possession on or about March 1, 199-. This is notice to you that you are using the premises for illegal or harmful purposes in that: You are using the premises for illegal gambling activities.

You are given three (3) days to vacate the premises.

If you fail to comply with this notice, unlawful detainer proceedings may be initiated against you.

DATED: June 27, 199-

10 Righteous Crescent, Anycity

TO: Thomas Tenant (tenant)
    Apt. 8 - 7 Renters' Avenue, Anycity

You occupy the premises located at Apt. 8 - 7 Renters' Avenue, Anycity under a month-to-month rental agreement. You are notified that the rental agreement is terminated effective June 30, 199-.

On that date you should have vacated the premises and removed all your belongings.

If you fail to comply with this notice, unlawful detainer proceedings may be initiated against you.

DATED: May 31, 199-

10 Renters' Avenue

directs the tenant to respond to the complaint on a date which is not less than six days or more than twelve days from the date the tenant receives it. The complaint accompanies the summons and states why the landlord believes the tenant should be evicted. Naturally, both documents must be in acceptable legal form. The act provides a summons form for evicting tenants as part of an unlawful detainer action.

Normally, the summons and complaint must be served personally on the tenant, but under some circumstances they may be posted on the premises and mailed to the tenant. Regardless of how the summons and complaint are received, the tenant should always consult a lawyer. If the tenant does not respond as directed, the landlord will obtain an eviction order by default.

(c) Writ of Restitution

At the time the summons and complaint are filed with the clerk of the superior court, the landlord may also get a court order directing the tenant to appear in court on the date provided in the summons or at a later date. At that time, the tenant would have to prove that there was no basis for the eviction action. For example, if the basis of the action were nonpayment of rent, the tenant would have to show that the rent was paid. If the tenant cannot provide adequate proof, the court will issue a Writ of Restitution. This is an order directing the county sheriff to physically remove the tenant and is the primary objective of the unlawful detainer action.

(d) Taking the tenant's personal property

At the time the writ of restitution is served by the sheriff, the landlord may enter the premises and take possession of the tenant's belongings. The belongings must then be stored in a secure place for eventual disposition. However, if the tenant objects to the landlord taking the property, the property must be placed "upon the nearest public property" and left for the tenant. If the tenant does not object or is not present when the writ of restitution is served by the sheriff, it will be presumed that the tenant agrees that the landlord should store the tenant's belongings, rather than removing them to public property. The tenant must be served with written notice explaining the tenant's right to object and the consequences of objecting to the landlord's storage of the tenant's property.

If the landlord stores the tenant's belongings, they must be returned to the tenant upon payment of what it cost the landlord to transport and store the property. If the tenant does not pay these costs, the landlord may sell the property. If the property is worth more than $50, it may be sold 45 days after giving the tenant written notice of intent to sell. However, the landlord may not sell the tenant's "personal papers, family pictures, and keepsakes." If the property is worth less than $50, it may be sold seven days after giving the tenant written notice of intent to sell. Income from the sale of the tenant's property must be applied to the landlord's costs of moving and storing the property. Any excess must be held for the tenant for a year, and if the tenant does not claim this money, it must be given to the State as abandoned property.

Note that the process described here is somewhat different from the process to be followed by a landlord when the tenant abandons property. Property is abandoned when the tenant intentionally leaves the property after vacating the premises. A discussion of how abandoned tenant property is to be handled is found in chapter 8.

(e) Trial

If the tenant can show a possible defense, the Writ of Restitution will be denied and a trial date will be set. Even if the writ is granted, the tenant still has a right to have a trial. However, the tenant will have to give up possession of the premises before the trial. At the trial, which can be either a jury trial or trial before a judge, the landlord must prove the existence of a rental agreement (oral and written), that proper notice was given, and that there is a legal basis to evict the tenant. If the landlord wins, a Writ of Restitution will be issued. Whenever the writ is issued, the landlord will also be entitled to a judgment against the tenant for any damages suffered, rent owing, court costs, and attorney's fees. If the tenant wins, the court will award the tenant court costs and attorney's fees.

(f) Defenses

The defenses available to a tenant in an unlawful detainer action are limited. If the landlord claims that rent has not been paid, the tenant must be able to show it was paid. This usually requires producing receipts or canceled checks. If the landlord claims that the tenant has not fulfilled any of the tenant's duties, the tenant must show that there has been substantial compliance. This means that the tenant, in good faith, has done most of what the landlord required. If the landlord claims that the tenant is acting illegally or damaging the property, the tenant must counter those specific allegations.

If the basis of the unlawful detainer action is a 20-day termination notice, one can only base one's defense on whether or not the notice was in the proper form and whether or not it was served properly. A landlord does not need any reason to terminate a month-to-month or periodic tenancy. This would not be true in Seattle where a defense might include failure to comply with the Seattle Just Cause Ordinance. Virtually all evictions from premises located within the City of Seattle can be contested since the landlord must prove there is cause or a reason for the eviction.

A tenant may not want to contest the landlord's claim to possession, but may have damage claims against the landlord. For example, the landlord may have damaged some of the tenant's property. If the tenant returns the premises before trial, the eviction action may be converted into a broader lawsuit, permitting the tenant's claims to be determined. Consult an attorney for this complex procedure.

One additional defense might be that the eviction action has been brought as a retaliation against the tenant for exercising his or her rights under the Landlord-Tenant Act. (This defense will be discussed in chapter 8.) These are very general defenses and there may be other more specific defenses depending on the situation. A lawyer should be consulted.

(g) Bonds

After a Writ of Restitution (a court eviction order) is issued, the landlord must obtain a bond for an amount sufficiently large to pay all court costs and any damages suffered by the tenant if it is determined at some later time that the writ was improperly issued. The writ is then delivered to the sheriff. In addition the sheriff will also require that a bond be obtained to protect the sheriff against a lawsuit by the tenant if the tenant ultimately proves that the writ should not have been issued and should not have been served by the sheriff. The sheriff enforces the Writ of Restitution by forcing the tenant to leave the premises. The sheriff is not responsible for moving the tenant's belongings.

(h) Stopping or delaying the Writ of Restitution

A tenant who is being evicted for not paying rent can delay or prevent the enforcement of a Writ of Restitution. If the writ is issued before trial, the tenant can pay all rent claimed by the landlord, plus accruing rental payments and court costs. This will allow the tenant to keep possession until there is a trial. If the writ is issued after a trial, its execution can be prevented if the tenant pays the amount of the judgment within five days of the trial. This can be done only if the term of tenancy has not expired.

d. SUMMARY

If the tenants do not perform the duties described in chapter 6, landlords have three remedies. They may have the repairs done and bill the tenants for the costs incurred, or they may seek judgment or arbitration awards compelling the tenants to comply with the landlords' requests or to provide them with money for damages. Finally, landlords may evict tenants. With one exception, no matter what remedy landlords seek, however, they must first give their tenants written notice and an opportunity to respond. The exception relates to tenants who engage in illegal drug activities or who are a danger to other tenants. The landlord may, without prior notice, evict tenants involved in these kinds of activities.

An unlawful detainer action is the only method used to evict a tenant. Because it is a complex lawsuit requiring special notices and involving bonds, a Writ of Restitution, and technical defenses, a lawyer should be consulted to initiate or defend against such a lawsuit.

8

COMMON PROBLEMS:
DAMAGE DEPOSITS,
RIGHT TO PRIVACY, AND OTHERS

Some problems have always accompanied the landlord-tenant relationship. How does a tenant terminate a tenancy? Can a landlord keep or dispose of property abandoned by a tenant? Should a landlord return or keep a tenant's damage deposit? Does a landlord have the right to enter the tenant's premises at any time? Can a landlord evict a tenant after the tenant has complained to government housing authorities that the premises are substandard? This chapter will answer these questions and will also examine arbitration as an alternative method for settling landlord-tenant disputes.

a. TERMINATING A MONTH-TO-MONTH TENANCY

Both the landlord and the tenant can terminate a month-to-month or any other kind of periodic tenancy by giving notice of termination. The notice must be in writing and contain the date the tenancy is to end. The termination date and the date the notice is delivered must be 20 days or more before the end of a monthly or other rent-paying period.

Thus in a month-to-month tenancy with rent payable on the first of each month, a termination notice would have to be received 20 days or more before the end of the month. The termination date could be the first day of the next month or any date thereafter. Sample #11 is an example of a notice to terminate.

SAMPLE #11
TWENTY-DAY NOTICE TERMINATING TENANCY
(By the tenant)

TO: Laurence Landlord (landlord)
     10 Tenancy Crescent

I occupy the premises located at Apt. 123-45 Rental Boulevard under a month-to-month rental agreement. You are notifed that the rental agreement is terminated effective April 30, 199- . On that date, I will be vacating the premises.

DATED: April 10, 199-

Apt. 123-45 Rental Boulevard

If the landlord decides to convert to a condominium type of ownership, or if the landlord adopts a policy of excluding children, a tenant affected by such changes is entitled to 90 days' written notice of termination before the landlord can implement these changes.

A City of Seattle ordinance (Seattle Housing Code 22.206.150) creates special termination notice requirements for tenants living within the city limits. The ordinance requires that written reasons for termination be given a month-to-month tenant before the tenancy can be terminated.

b. ABANDONED PROPERTY

A related problem arises when the tenant leaves without giving the 20-day written termination notice. If the tenant owes rent and the landlord has reason to believe that the tenant is going to abandon or has abandoned the premises, the tenant will have to pay the following rent:

> (1) When the tenancy is month-to-month, the tenant shall be liable for the rent for the thirty days following either the date the landlord learns of the abandonment, or the date the next regular rental payment would have become due, whichever first occurs.
>
> (2) When the tenancy is for a term greater than month-to-month, the tenant shall be liable for the lesser of the following:
>
>> (a) The entire rent due for the remainder of the term; or
>>
>> (b) All rent accrued during the period reasonably necessary to rerent the premises at a fair rental, plus the difference between such fair rental and the rent agreed to in the prior agreement.

If the tenant breaks a long-term rental agreement, the tenant will not only be responsible for the rent owing until the premises are rerented, but will also have to pay the landlord's costs incurred in rerenting, and reasonable attorney's fees.

However, this obligation will be reduced and perhaps eliminated if the landlord does not make a reasonable effort to rerent the premises. This is known as a duty to mitigate (or lessen) damages.

After the tenant has abandoned the premises, the landlord may enter immediately. If the tenant has left any property, the landlord may take it and store it in a reasonably secure place. The landlord must then make a reasonable effort to provide the tenant with a written notice containing the landlord's name and address, the location of the stored property, the date the landlord intends to sell the property, and the right of the tenant to get the property back. At least 45 days after sending this notice, the landlord may sell the property as indicated in the notice sent to the tenant. If the value of the property is less than $50, the landlord must wait only 7 days after notifying the tenant before disposing of the belongings. However, a tenant's personal papers, family pictures, and keepsakes may not be disposed of until 45 days after notification, even if the value is under $50.

The proceeds from the sale may be used by the landlord to pay all rent owing and storage and transportation costs. Any excess money must be held by the landlord for one year from the date of the sale and may then be kept if the tenant does not claim it.

c. PRE-OCCUPANCY, SECURITY, AND DAMAGE DEPOSITS

The question of what happens to deposits made by tenants has been the basis for many disputes. The Landlord-Tenant Act offers a cure. The Act recognizes three types of deposits: pre-occupancy deposits, damage deposits and security deposits. None of these deposits may be collected or kept without a written agreement specifying the conditions under which the deposit is obtained. In the case of damage and security deposits, the landlord must provide the tenant with a written checklist describing the condition and cleanliness of the premises at the beginning of the tenancy. The checklist must be signed and dated by both the landlord and tenant and the tenant must be given a copy.

The pre-occupancy deposit is required by some landlords to put prospective tenants on a waiting list for the next available unit. The landlord must give the prospective tenant a receipt for the deposit as well as a written statement of how the money is to be used. If the tenant occupies the unit, the deposit must either be applied to the first month's rent or it may be used as a security deposit. If the unit is not occupied, the landlord may keep the deposit only if the written statement provided with the receipt permits this result. If there is no such written statement, the landlord must return the entire amount of the deposit. If the landlord does not comply, the landlord is subject to a penalty of up to $100 and payment of court costs and attorney fees.

Related to the pre-occupancy deposit are the costs associated with tenant screening. A landlord may charge a reasonable fee for these costs provided the prospective tenant is notified in writing. This writing must state what the tenant screening entails, inform the prospective tenant of the right to dispute the information developed and identify any tenant screening service to be used. Tenant screening costs may include long distance phone calls and time spent checking references. A landlord not providing the required notice is subject to a penalty of up to $100 and payment of court costs and attorney fees.

A damage deposit may only be used to pay for damage to the premises that the tenant has caused negligently or intentionally. (An example might be a broken window or a hole burned in a carpet.) The damage deposit may not be used to pay for "normal wear and tear resulting from the ordinary use of the premises." This would include faded paint on the walls or an old appliance that wore out.

The security deposit is used to ensure that the tenant will perform the obligations specified in the rental agreement. The deposit may not be kept upon termination of the tenancy unless there is a previous written rental agreement between the parties, stating all the conditions under which the landlord may keep the deposit. Many rental agreements allow the landlord to keep a security deposit if the tenant leaves prior to the termination date of the tenancy.

To be distinguished from both the damage and security deposits is the nonrefundable fee. Some landlords require tenants to pay for cleaning, painting, or minor repairs. This practice is permitted only if a written rental agreement clearly states that money paid by the tenants is nonrefundable and is to be used for such purposes.

In summary, if a landlord receives a deposit from a tenant, the landlord must clearly indicate in a written rental agreement whether it is a security or damage deposit. The agreement must state the conditions under which the security deposit will be kept. If a damage deposit is made, the agreement must state whether a portion of it will be kept to clean the premises.

The landlord must keep all moneys paid by the tenant as a deposit, in a trust account in "a bank, savings and loan association, mutual savings bank or licensed escrow agent located in Washington." The landlord must give the tenant a written receipt for the deposit and written notification of the name and address of the institution holding the deposit. If the location is changed, the tenant must receive notice of the change. Any interest generated on the deposit may be kept by the landlord unless the rental agreement contains some other arrangement.

Once the tenant has vacated the premises, the landlord must send a written notice to the tenant that the deposit or a portion of it will be kept. The notice must be sent within 14 days after the tenant has left and it must give "full and specific statement" of the reasons for keeping the deposit. If the landlord does not follow these steps, the landlord may have to pay the tenant up to two times the amount of the deposit, as well as the tenant's court costs and attorney's fees. In addition, the landlord may lose the right to collect any money for damages caused by the tenant. Of course, if the proper notice is given, the tenant is still responsible for all damages to the property, and these may be collected by the landlord even if they exceed the amount of the deposit.

d. RIGHT TO ENTER THE TENANT'S PREMISES

The Landlord-Tenant Act gives tenants a limited right of privacy. While the landlord may not enter the premises without notice or a valid reason, neither may the tenant unreasonably exclude the landlord. Both landlord and tenant may be subject to penalties for violations of their respective duties. The act provides:

> (1) The tenant shall not unreasonably withhold consent to the landlord to enter into the dwelling unit in order to inspect the premises, make necessary or agreed repairs, alterations, or improvements, supply necessary or agreed services, or exhibit the dwelling unit to prospective or actual purchasers, mortgagees, tenants, workmen, or contractors.

> (2) The landlord may enter the dwelling unit without consent of the tenant in case of emergency or abandonment.

> (3) The landlord shall not abuse the right of access or use it to harass the tenant. Except in the case of emergency or if it is impractical to do so, the landlord shall give the tenant at least two days' notice of his intent to enter and shall enter only at reasonable times. The tenant shall not unreasonably withhold consent to the landlord to enter the dwelling unit at a specified time where the landlord has given at least one day's notice of intent to enter to exhibit the dwelling unit to prospective or actual purchasers or tenants. A landlord shall not unreasonably interfere with a tenant's enjoyment of the rented dwelling unit by excessive exhibiting of the dwelling unit.

> (4) The landlord has no other right of access except by court order, arbitration, or by consent of the tenant.

> (5) A landlord or tenant who continues to violate this section after being served with one written notification alleging good faith violation of this section and listing the date and time of the violation shall be liable for up to one hundred dollars for each violation after receipt of the notice. The prevailing party may recover costs of the suit or arbitration under this section and may also recover reasonable attorney's fees.

The act attempts to balance the rights of both tenants and landlords as to the right of entry. Normally, the tenant may insist that the landlord may not come into the premises without consent. When consent is given, the landlord may not abuse that consent. Thus if the landlord is permitted to show the premises to a prospective tenant, the landlord may not stay longer than necessary nor use it as an opportunity to embarrass or harass the tenant. Of course, the landlord would not need consent to enter in the case of an emergency like a fire or if the tenant has abandoned the premises.

Although the tenant can insist that the landlord first obtain consent to enter, the tenant should be cautious about refusing the landlord entry. If the tenant unreasonably withholds consent, that can have undesirable consequences for the tenant. For example, if the tenant has asked the landlord to make repairs and then denies the landlord access, the tenant may lose the right to insist that the repairs be made. Or if the tenant refuses to let the landlord show the premises to a prospective tenant, the landlord may be able to get a court order and the tenant may have to pay the landlord damages. The key word for both landlord and tenant is "reasonable."

If either the landlord or the tenant believes that the other has violated this section of the act, a remedy is provided. Written notice of the claimed violation must be given and thereafter a penalty of up to $100 for each subsequent violation may be awarded by a court or arbitrator. This means that if the landlord made an authorized entry into the tenant's apartment, the tenant must inform the landlord in writing of the unauthorized entry and demand it not recur. Should the landlord ignore the notice and again make an unauthorized entry, the tenant may claim the $100 penalty under this section.

e. RETALIATION BY THE LANDLORD

The Landlord-Tenant Act anticipates that some landlords might retaliate against tenants seeking to exercise their rights under the act. Human nature being what it is, it may well be much easier to replace a complaining tenant than do the necessary repairs. However, the act says that a landlord may not retaliate against a tenant when the tenant complains about the condition of the premises to a governmental authority.

The act says retaliation —

> ....shall mean and include but not be limited to any of the following actions by the landlord when such actions are intended primarily to retaliate against a tenant because of the tenant's good faith and lawful act:
>
> (1) Eviction of the tenant;
> (2) Increasing the rent required of the tenant;
> (3) Reduction of services to the tenant;
> (4) Increasing the obligations of the tenant.

Previously, there was a presumption of retaliation if the landlord took any kind of adverse action against the tenant after a complaint had been filed. Thus, if the landlord took any of the actions described above, it was presumed that the landlord was unlawfully retaliating against the tenant. That presumption has now been limited.

There is no presumption of retaliation if the tenant complains of a condition which does not "endanger or impair the health or safety of the tenant." Nor is there a presumption of retaliation if at the time of filing the complaint, the tenant owes rent or has not complied with any other lease or rental obligations as described in chapter 6. In that instance, there is a presumption that the landlord has not retaliated against the tenant.

Of course these limitations do not mean that the landlord did not retaliate, they mean only that the tenant has the primary burden of proof. This may be a very difficult burden if the tenant files the complaint after the landlord has raised the rent or taken some other action which might or might not have been done in good faith.

Moreover, if a landlord takes any of those adverse actions within 90 days after a government agency has inspected or started enforcement proceedings against the premises, it will be presumed that the landlord has violated this section. The landlord may rebut the presumption by showing that the premises can't be repaired while the tenant remains in possession. In an instance where the rent has been increased, the landlord must show that the tenant had previously been given a notice which specified reasonable grounds for the rent increase.

Violation of this section will give the tenant a defense to an unlawful detainer action and will require the landlord to pay the tenant's court costs and a reasonable attorney's fee in any court proceedings.

f. HOLDING THE TENANT'S PROPERTY

At one time landlords could lawfully hold a tenant's personal belongings to ensure the tenant would pay rent that was owing. The act makes this unlawful and even makes unlawful a provision in a rental agreement which would seem to give the landlord this right to retain the tenant's property.

Should a landlord violate this section of the act, the tenant is provided with a most effective remedy. First, the tenant must write to the landlord demanding that the tenant's property be immediately returned, If the landlord refuses, the landlord is liable not only for the value of the property retained, but also for damages of up to $100 per day (not to exceed $1,000) as well as the tenant's attorney's fees.

g. ARBITRATION

Arbitration, as I mentioned in the introduction, is an informal dispute settling proceeding which consists of a person or persons who are authorized to render a final binding decision. These persons may be lawyers but are not judges. Arbitration, which can only be used if both parties agree to it in writing, is relatively inexpensive and tends to produce decisions much more quickly than court proceedings. Usually technical rules of evidence are relaxed, making it easier for inexperienced parties to present their cases. Both tenants and landlords may find that it is much more accessible and much more inexpensive than court proceedings, particularly for those disputes which are relatively minor and involve small amounts of money. The parties are free to agree about what fees should be assessed in an arbitration proceeding.

An alternative to arbitration is mediation. It differs from arbitration in that a mediator's decision is not binding. As with arbitration, both parties would have to agree to submit their dispute to this process.

h. DISPLACED LOW INCOME TENANTS

Under some circumstances, low income tenants who lose their housing to development may be entitled to relocation assistance. This includes moving expenses, advance rental and deposit payments for new housing, advance utility deposits, and rent and utility payment subsidies for a year. Relocation assistance is only available in municipalities that have adopted a relocation assistance plan. These plans are quite complex and each municipality must meet eligibility standards. Landlords or tenants finding themselves in this situation should consult the department of community development of their local government for details.

i. SUMMARY

The Landlord-Tenant Act attempts to deal with those problems that have always beset landlords and tenants. To terminate a tenancy the tenant must give written notice and if it is not done properly, the tenant will be responsible for rent after leaving the premises. If a tenant leaves personal property on the premises, the landlord may be able to sell it if he or she follows several procedural steps. Deposits must be characterized in writing by the landlord as being either security or damage deposits. (Each has a different purpose.)

A landlord may not keep a deposit unless it is used for an authorized purpose and unless the tenant is given notice.

Unless there is an emergency or the tenant has abandoned the premises, the landlord must get consent before entering a tenant's premises. The tenant should not exclude the landlord unreasonably. The landlord may not retaliate against a tenant who has attempted to force the landlord to perform the landlord's duties (as described in chapter 4). Retaliation includes the initiation of eviction proceedings and even increasing the rent. Under no circumstances may the landlord retain a tenant's personal property as a means of collecting rent. Finally, arbitration or mediation may be an inexpensive, expeditious way to settle landlord-tenant disputes and should be considered by both parties.

Tenants who lose their housing to development may be entitled to financial assistance. The department of community development of the local city or county should be consulted for details.

9
FAIR HOUSING LAWS

A landlord may be discriminating in selecting a tenant as long as a tenant is not discriminated against because of race, color, religion, sex, national origin, and, in some instances, handicap and familial status. Laws prohibiting discrimination in housing (fair housing laws) emanate from every level of government. They cover housing sales and housing rentals. The fair housing laws are similar in that all have agencies to receive and investigate complaints. However, they differ in the types of housing they cover, the types of acts they prohibit, and in the extent to which they permit access to the courts.

a. FEDERAL LAW (TITLE VIII)

The federal fair housing law is Title VIII of the Civil Rights Act of 1968. Title VIII prohibits discrimination because of race, color, religion, sex, handicap or disability, familial status, or national origin. It prohibits the following actions:

(a) A refusal to rent

(b) Discriminatory terms and conditions in rental agreements

(c) Discriminatory advertising

(d) Making misleading statements as to the availability of housing

(e) "Blockbusting" or inducing owners to rent or sell by telling them that persons of a certain race or other protected classes are about to enter the neighborhood.

Housing discrimination based on disability includes discrimination based on a need to accommodate a tenant's disabilities. For example, a tenant may require an entry ramp for wheelchair access or specially designed appliances. A landlord may not refuse to rent to a tenant requiring reasonable accommodations when the tenant will make the accommodations at his or her own expense. Multifamily dwellings first occupied after 1990 may be required to be accessible by tenants with disabilities along with other construction features making them adaptable to tenants with special needs.

Nevertheless, Title VIII does not apply to four situations. The owner of the single family house is not covered if the owner does not own more than three such houses at any one time and if the owner does not use professional real estate sales or rental people to assist in its rental.

The owner of the multi-room or unit dwelling (boarding house) is also not covered if not more than four families occupy it at any one time and if the owner is the occupant of some of the rooms or units.

Religious organizations are not covered if occupancy is limited to their members and if the membership is not restricted by race, color, and national origin.

The familial status limitation (head of household with one or more children under the age of 18) does not apply to housing limited to occupancy by older people.

Persons with complaints have two remedies. They may file a written complaint with the secretary of Housing and Urban Development within one year after the alleged discriminatory act. Within 10 days of receiving the complaint, the department must notify the accused of the complaint and within 100 days the department must complete its investigation or notify the complainant why more time is needed. If reasonable cause is found to support the complaint, then an administrative hearing may be held. Alternatively, the complaining party may choose not to ask for help from the Secretary of Housing and Urban Development and simply file a lawsuit. Such a lawsuit would have to be filed within two years of the alleged discrimination.

Under some circumstances a court may appoint an attorney for the complainant. Available relief may include an injunction, actual and punitive damages, court costs, and reasonable attorney fees.

b. STATE LAW PROHIBITING DISCRIMINATION

The state law prohibiting discrimination is broader than Title VIII. It prohibits discrimination based on "race, creed, color, national origin, sex, marital status, age, or the presence of any sensory, mental or physical handicap." The state law covers the selling, renting, and advertising of real estate.

Complaints may be filed with the State Human Rights Commission, but must be filed within six months after the alleged act of discrimination. The commission investigates the complaint and makes preliminary findings. If the complaint is not resolved, the commission can hold a hearing and provide administrative relief. The commission's decisions can be appealed to the superior court. A complaining party may avoid the state agency and file a lawsuit in superior court. Remedies for either approach include an injunction, damages, and attorneys' fees. An attorney should be consulted for advice as to the time limitations on filing a lawsuit in superior court.

c. SEATTLE OPEN HOUSING ORDINANCE

The Seattle Open Housing Ordinance (City of Seattle Ordinance No. 104839) is offered here as an example of a local law prohibiting discrimination. Local laws will vary and each local jurisdiction should be consulted. The significant difference in the Seattle Ordinance is that it adds "sexual orientation" and "political ideology" to the list of protected classes. Section 2(14) defines "political ideology" as:

> ...any idea or belief, or coordinated body of ideas or beliefs, relating to the conduct, organization, function, or basis of government and related institutions and activities, whether or not characteristic of any political party or group. This term includes membership or participation in the activities of a group with shared political ideology, provided such membership or participation does not involve force or violence or produce or incite imminent force or violence toward persons or property.

Section 2(22) defines sexual orientation as:

> ...male or female heterosexuality, bi-sexuality or homosexuality, and includes a person's attitudes, preferences, beliefs and practices pertaining to sex, but shall not include conduct which is unlawful under city, state, or federal law.

In 1979 the ordinance was amended to expand protected classes to include "parental status," which means being a "parent, step-parent, adoptive parent, guardian, foster parent, or custodian of a minor child or children, which child or children shall permanently or temporarily occupy the real estate." Thus a Seattle landlord may not discriminate against people with children.

Complaints must be filed within six months from the date of the alleged discriminatory act. They must be filed with the Department of Human Rights unless the charge involves sex, marital status, or sexual orientation, in which case it should be filed with the Office of Women's Rights. If the complaint is not resolved, a hearing can be held and administrative relief granted. There is no provision for private enforcement.

d. SUMMARY

It may be that a tenant would have a claim against a landlord under all three types of laws. As it usually does not require the services of an attorney, it is wise to file charges with all three levels of government. There is no cost, and the kind of response and the time it takes to get action will vary with the individual agencies. Alternatively, secure the assistance of a lawyer and obtain advice regarding the desirability of filing litigation.

For landlords the message is clear: do not discriminate! If prospective tenants are rejected, then it must be for reasons other than those prohibited by the fair housing laws. It is legitimate for a landlord to be concerned about a party's ability to pay rent and whether a party will care for the landlord's property properly.

The problems arise when these legitimate concerns become mixed with personal feelings. In those cases, the landlord will lose.

Fair housing laws affect all landlords and tenants. The duty not to discriminate is well established at every level of government. Fair housing laws do not require a landlord to rent to everyone. They simply prevent a landlord from rejecting a tenant for the reasons prohibited by laws.

10
ANSWERS TO YOUR QUESTIONS

You now know what the Landlord-Tenant Act is about. Whether you are a landlord or a tenant, you know you have rights and responsibilities even if you did not bargain for them. This knowledge should assist you in the creation and maintenance of a satisfactory landlord-tenant relationship. But honest differences develop from even the best relationships, and sometimes they escalate into arguments, the expenditure of attorney fees, and perhaps the dissolution of the landlord-tenant relationship.

It has been my experience that there are several areas that cause most of the problems for the landlord-tenant relationship. Not all are easily solved from a reading of the Landlord-Tenant Act. This chapter considers some of the more common problem areas and offers solutions.

a. WHAT IF THERE IS NO WRITTEN RENTAL AGREEMENT?

This question is usually asked after the tenant brings a baby lion into the apartment or after the landlord removes all the curtains. You will remember that the Landlord-Tenant Act requires a written rental agreement only if the tenancy is to exceed one year. But that should not be interpreted to mean that you do not otherwise *need* a written agreement.

A written rental agreement will not solve all disputes. It will, however, go a long way toward reducing disputes over the items covered in the agreement. Without one, you are inviting a war over who has the best memory. If a promise is worth making, it is worth putting in writing. If the landlord-tenant relationship is worth entering into, it is worth formalizing in a written document. If you do not have a written rental agreement, you are foolish, and you are putting more trust in your luck and in the fates than this book would recommend.

b. WHAT IF I WANT TO KEEP THE LANDLORD OUT?

The Landlord-Tenant Act requires a landlord to respect a tenant's privacy. It prohibits a landlord from entering the premises without prior notice or tenant consent unless the tenant has abandoned the premises or there is an emergency. This is a basic statement of the tenant's right to keep the landlord out. In one case, this led a tenant to change the locks on the doors and refuse to give a key to the landlord.

The answer is that both parties must be reasonable. The landlord is the owner of the property, and the tenant has a right of use. The landlord retains a continuing interest in the condition of the premises. The tenant has a right to insist that the premises be kept habitable, and that will require the landlord to have reasonable access.

Clearly, the landlord can be excluded when entry is sought for reasons other than those permitted by the act. But it is equally clear that the tenant may be waiving landlord obligations by arbitrarily denying entry as well as creating a needless strain in the landlord-tenant relationship.

c. WHAT IF THE LANDLORD WANTS TO INCREASE THE RENT OR MAKE OTHER CHANGES IN THE TENANCY ARRANGEMENT?

The Landlord-Tenant Act does not limit what may be charged for rent. Unless the rental agreement provides otherwise, a landlord can increase the rent at any time during the tenancy.

The act requires only that the landlord give written notice 30 days prior to the effective date of the rent increase.

Not only can the landlord increase the rent, but he or she can change other tenancy terms and conditions as well. New restrictions could be placed on pets, deposits could be increased, or other rules of occupancy could be changed. This is another good reason for the parties to have a written rental agreement. If there is agreement as to a fixed amount of rent for a definite period or as to the other conditions of occupancy, then that agreement cannot be changed without both parties agreeing to it.

d. WHAT IF THE LANDLORD SELLS?

A tenant has the right to possess and use property owned by a landlord. As long as that relationship exists, no one can interfere with the tenant's possession. If a landlord sells, the sale is subject to the tenant's interest in the property. If the tenant has a long-term rental agreement, the new owner must honor it. If the tenant has no rental agreement or a month-to-month tenancy, the new owner may terminate the tenancy by giving a proper written eviction notice.

e. WHAT IF I HAVE BEEN A GOOD TENANT AND THE LANDLORD WANTS TO EVICT ME?

A tenancy established by oral agreement or a month-to-month tenancy can be terminated for any lawful reasons. The unlawful reasons include the kinds of discrimination described in chapter 9 and retaliation against a tenant for exercising rights created by the Landlord-Tenant Act.

If the landlord uses the 20-day written eviction notice procedure, no reason for the eviction need be given. However, a long-term rental agreement (more than one year) cannot be terminated without adequate reasons. Adequate reasons include violations of any of the rental agreement provisions.

f. WHAT IF THE RENT IS NOT PAID ON TIME?

Rent is ordinarily paid on a monthly basis, and if not paid once a month, it is a basis for eviction. A common problem is when there is no agreement on the payment date. In such a case a tenant will not be in default as long as rent is paid some time each month. When the rental agreement provides for a payment date, the tenant will be in default on the day following that date. Even though a payment date is set, a landlord may waive the right to receive payment on that date by regularly accepting the belated payments.

g. WHAT IF A RENT PAYMENT IS ACCEPTED AFTER A THREE-DAY NOTICE IS SERVED ON THE TENANT?

A three-day notice states alternatively that either all rent owing must be paid within three days or the tenant must vacate. The notice must state the exact amount of rent owing; if, within the three-day period, that amount is paid, the landlord must accept it.

The landlord does not have to accept the rent if offered after the three-day period, or if the amount of rent offered is less than that stated in the notice. If, under these circumstances, the rent is accepted and the landlord waives the three-day notice, the tenant will be allowed to stay and the landlord will have to serve another notice.

h. WHAT IF THE DAMAGE IS CAUSED BY SOMEONE ELSE?

Damage deposits have always been the source of landlord-tenant disputes. Frequently the issue is whether damage was caused by a prior tenant, rather than the present tenant. A relatively simple procedure may help. Immediately upon taking possession, the tenant should inspect the premises, making a written record of any damage, painting and cleaning needs and required repairs (see Sample #2).

This record should be reviewed with the landlord for possible corrective action and to obtain acknowledgment of the items noted. It would be advisable for both parties to sign the document and for the tenant to give a copy to the landlord. When the tenant vacates, the condition of the premises can be compared with the previously prepared record. If the landlord is not present when the premises are vacated, the tenant should have a witness to verify its condition.

The preprinted form provided in Self-Counsel's *Rental Form Kit* is a good example of the kind of record both the landlord and tenant should have.

i. WHAT IF THE TENANT WANTS TO RENT SUBSTANDARD HOUSING AND FIX IT UP?

A major reason for enacting the Landlord-Tenant Act was to make it unlawful to rent substandard housing. As a practical matter, there may be instances where a skilled tenant is willing to make repairs in return for a rent credit or other compensation. As long as that work is completed before the tenant moves in, the act is not violated. However, the act prohibits a tenant from living in substandard housing, so the tenant may not live in it while making repairs. Of course, this does not apply to repairs needed during the tenancy, as the act provides procedures for these repairs.

The one exception (RCW 59.18.360) to the prohibition against renting substandard housing requires a carefully drawn written agreement approved by the tenant's attorney or public officials. It is doubtful such approval will be easily obtained.

j. WHAT IF THE LANDLORD WANTS TO CONVERT TO A CONDOMINIUM?

In larger cities, condominium conversions are quite popular. Unfortunately, these conversions frequently displace tenants who are unable or unwilling to purchase a condominium unit. In response, some cities have adopted condominium ordinances which limit or place conditions on conversions. The ordinances vary and should be consulted. In 1979, the Washington Legislature passed a law requiring a landlord to give written notice of an intended conversion 90 days prior to terminating the tenancy. This must be used instead of the 20-day written notice.

k.   WHAT IF A LANDLORD CUTS OFF A TENANT'S UTILITY SERVICES?

Eviction proceedings can be expensive and time consuming. At one time, some landlords sought to avoid the formal eviction process by simply having the tenant's utility services terminated. In most cases this tactic was quite successful as the tenant vacated quickly. However, the act expressly prohibits this practice. A landlord intentionally causing a tenant to be without water, heat, electricity, or gas may have to pay a tenant up to $100 a day, plus actual damages suffered by the tenant, including the tenant's attorney fees. Of course, a landlord may have to interrupt a tenant's utility services for purposes of repair, but the period of time must be reasonable and it cannot be used to harass or force the tenant to vacate. If a landlord intends to evict a tenant, the formal eviction procedures must be used and a lawyer consulted.

l.   SUMMARY

It usually takes two people to cause a dispute. That should mean that one person can prevent one. This chapter discussed common landlord-tenant disagreements. It illustrated that many of these disputes can be eliminated by thoughtful planning on the part of either the landlord or the tenant.

APPENDIX
RESIDENTIAL LANDLORD-TENANT ACT

RCW 59.18.010 Short title. RCW 59.18.010 through 59.18.420 and 59.18.900 shall be known and may be cited as the "Residential Landlord-Tenant Act of 1973", and shall constitute a new chapter in Title 59 RCW. [1973 1st ex.s. c 207 § 1.]

RCW 59.18.020 Rights and remedies--Obligation of good faith imposed. Every duty under this chapter and every act which must be performed as a condition precedent to the exercise of a right or remedy under this chapter imposes an obligation of good faith in its performance or enforcement. [1973 1st ex.s. c 207 § 2.]

RCW 59.18.030 Definitions. As used in this chapter:
(1) "Dwelling unit" is a structure or that part of a structure which is used as a home, residence, or sleeping place by one person or by two or more persons maintaining a common household, including but not limited to single family residences and units of multiplexes, apartment buildings, and mobile homes.
(2) "Landlord" means the owner, lessor, or sublessor of the dwelling unit or the property of which it is a part, and in addition means any person designated as representative of the landlord.
(3) "Person" means an individual, group of individuals, corporation, government, or governmental agency, business trust, estate, trust, partnership, or association, two or more persons having a joint or common interest, or any other legal or commercial entity.
(4) "Owner" means one or more persons, jointly or severally, in whom is vested:
(a) All or any part of the legal title to property; or
(b) All or part of the beneficial ownership, and a right to present use and enjoyment of the property.
(5) "Premises" means a dwelling unit, appurtenances thereto, grounds, and facilities held out for the use of tenants generally and any other area or facility which is held out for use by the tenant.
(6) "Rental agreement" means all agreements which establish or modify the terms, conditions, rules, regulations, or any other provisions concerning the use and occupancy of a dwelling unit.
(7) A "single family residence" is a structure maintained and used as a single dwelling unit. Notwithstanding that a dwelling unit shares one or more walls with another dwelling unit, it shall be deemed a single family residence if it has direct access to a street and shares neither heating facilities nor hot water equipment, nor any other essential facility or service, with any other dwelling unit.
(8) A "tenant" is any person who is entitled to occupy a dwelling unit primarily for living or dwelling purposes under a rental agreement.
(9) "Reasonable attorney's fees", where authorized in this chapter, means an amount to be determined including the following factors: The time and labor required, the novelty and difficulty of the questions involved, the skill requisite to perform the legal service properly, the fee customarily charged in the locality for similar legal services, the amount involved and the results obtained, and the experience, reputation and ability of the lawyer or lawyers performing the services.
(10) "Gang" means a group that: (a) Consists of three or more persons; (b) has identifiable leadership or an identifiable name, sign, or symbol; and (c) on an ongoing basis, regularly conspires and acts in concert mainly for criminal purposes.
(11) "Gang-related activity" means any activity that occurs within the gang or advances a gang purpose. [1998 c 276 § 1; 1973 1st ex.s. c 207 § 3.]

Please note that this act changes frequently, so you should not rely solely on the wording that appears here.

RCW 59.18.040 Living arrangements exempted from chapter. The following living arrangements are not intended to be governed by the provisions of this chapter, unless established primarily to avoid its application, in which event the provisions of this chapter shall control:

(1) Residence at an institution, whether public or private, where residence is merely incidental to detention or the provision of medical, religious, educational, recreational, or similar services, including but not limited to correctional facilities, licensed nursing homes, monasteries and convents, and hospitals;

(2) Occupancy under a bona fide earnest money agreement to purchase or contract of sale of the dwelling unit or the property of which it is a part, where the tenant is, or stands in the place of, the purchaser;

(3) Residence in a hotel, motel, or other transient lodging whose operation is defined in RCW 19.48.010;

(4) Rental agreements entered into pursuant to the provisions of chapter 47.12 RCW where occupancy is by an owner-condemnee and where such agreement does not violate the public policy of this state of ensuring decent, safe, and sanitary housing and is so certified by the consumer protection division of the attorney general's office;

(5) Rental agreements for the use of any single family residence which are incidental to leases or rentals entered into in connection with a lease of land to be used primarily for agricultural purposes;

(6) Rental agreements providing housing for seasonal agricultural employees while provided in conjunction with such employment;

(7) Rental agreements with the state of Washington, department of natural resources, on public lands governed by Title 79 RCW;

(8) Occupancy by an employee of a landlord whose right to occupy is conditioned upon employment in or about the premises. [1989 c 342 § 3; 1973 1st ex.s. c 207 § 4.]

RCW 59.18.050 Jurisdiction of district and superior courts. The district or superior courts of this state may exercise jurisdiction over any landlord or tenant with respect to any conduct in this state governed by this chapter or with respect to any claim arising from a transaction subject to this chapter within the respective jurisdictions of the district or superior courts as provided in Article IV, section 6 of the Constitution of the state of Washington. [1973 1st ex.s. c 207 § 5.]

RCW 59.18.055 Notice--Alternative procedure--Court's jurisdiction limited--Application to chapter 59.20 RCW. (1) When the plaintiff, after the exercise of due diligence, is unable to personally serve the summons on the defendant, the court may authorize the alternative means of service described herein. Upon filing of an affidavit from the person or persons attempting service describing those attempts, and the filing of an affidavit from the plaintiff, plaintiff's agent, or plaintiff's attorney stating the belief that the defendant cannot be found, the court may enter an order authorizing service of the summons as follows:

(a) The summons and complaint shall be posted in a conspicuous place on the premises unlawfully held, not less than nine days from the return date stated in the summons; and

(b) Copies of the summons and complaint shall be deposited in the mail, postage prepaid, by both regular mail and certified mail directed to the defendant's or defendants' last known address not less than nine days from the return date stated in the summons.

When service on the defendant or defendants is accomplished by this alternative procedure, the court's jurisdiction is limited to restoring possession of the premises to the plaintiff and no money judgment may be entered against the defendant or defendants until such time as jurisdiction over the defendant or defendants is obtained.

(2) This section shall apply to this chapter and chapter 59.20 RCW. [1997 c 86 § 1; 1989 c 342 § 14.]

94

RCW 59.18.060 Landlord--Duties. The landlord will at all times during the tenancy keep the premises fit for human habitation, and shall in particular:

(1) Maintain the premises to substantially comply with any applicable code, statute, ordinance, or regulation governing their maintenance or operation, which the legislative body enacting the applicable code, statute, ordinance or regulation could enforce as to the premises rented if such condition substantially endangers or impairs the health or safety of the tenant;

(2) Maintain the roofs, floors, walls, chimneys, fireplaces, foundations, and all other structural components in reasonably good repair so as to be usable and capable of resisting any and all normal forces and loads to which they may be subjected;

(3) Keep any shared or common areas reasonably clean, sanitary, and safe from defects increasing the hazards of fire or accident;

(4) Provide a reasonable program for the control of infestation by insects, rodents, and other pests at the initiation of the tenancy and, except in the case of a single family residence, control infestation during tenancy except where such infestation is caused by the tenant;

(5) Except where the condition is attributable to normal wear and tear, make repairs and arrangements necessary to put and keep the premises in as good condition as it by law or rental agreement should have been, at the commencement of the tenancy;

(6) Provide reasonably adequate locks and furnish keys to the tenant;

(7) Maintain all electrical, plumbing, heating, and other facilities and appliances supplied by him in reasonably good working order;

(8) Maintain the dwelling unit in reasonably weathertight condition;

(9) Except in the case of a single family residence, provide and maintain appropriate receptacles in common areas for the removal of ashes, rubbish, and garbage, incidental to the occupancy and arrange for the reasonable and regular removal of such waste;

(10) Except where the building is not equipped for the purpose, provide facilities adequate to supply heat and water and hot water as reasonably required by the tenant;

(11) Provide a written notice to the tenant that the dwelling unit is equipped with a smoke detection device as required in RCW 48.48.140. The notice shall inform the tenant of the tenant's responsibility to maintain the smoke detection device in proper operating condition and of penalties for failure to comply with the provisions of RCW 48.48.140(3). The notice must be signed by the landlord or the landlord's authorized agent and tenant with copies provided to both parties.

(12) Designate to the tenant the name and address of the person who is the landlord by a statement on the rental agreement or by a notice conspicuously posted on the premises. The tenant shall be notified immediately of any changes by certified mail or by an updated posting. If the person designated in this section does not reside in the state where the premises are located, there shall also be designated a person who resides in the county who is authorized to act as an agent for the purposes of service of notices and process, and if no designation is made of a person to act as agent, then the person to whom rental payments are to be made shall be considered such agent.

No duty shall devolve upon the landlord to repair a defective condition under this section, nor shall any defense or remedy be available to the tenant under this chapter, where the defective condition complained of was caused by the conduct of such tenant, his family, invitee, or other person acting under his control, or where a tenant unreasonably fails to allow the landlord access to the property for purposes of repair. When the duty imposed by subsection (1) of this section is incompatible with and greater than the duty imposed by any other provisions of this section, the landlord's duty shall be determined pursuant to subsection (1) of this section. [1991 c 154 § 2; 1973 1st ex.s. c 207 § 6.]

RCW 59.18.063 Landlord--Provide written receipt upon request.
A landlord shall provide, upon the request of a tenant, a written
receipt for any payments made by the tenant. [1997 c 84 § 1.]

RCW 59.18.070 Landlord--Failure to perform duties--Notice
from tenant--Contents--Time limits for landlord's remedial action.
If at any time during the tenancy the landlord fails to carry out
the duties required by RCW 59.18.060 or by the rental agreement,
the tenant may, in addition to pursuit of remedies otherwise
provided him by law, deliver written notice to the person
designated in *RCW 59.18.060(11), or to the person who collects the
rent, which notice shall specify the premises involved, the name of
the owner, if known, and the nature of the defective condition.
The landlord shall commence remedial action after receipt of such
notice by the tenant as soon as possible but not later than the
following time periods, except where circumstances are beyond the
landlord's control:
      (1) Not more than twenty-four hours, where the defective
condition deprives the tenant of hot or cold water, heat, or
electricity, or is imminently hazardous to life;
      (2) Not more than seventy-two hours, where the defective
condition deprives the tenant of the use of a refrigerator, range
and oven, or a major plumbing fixture supplied by the landlord; and
      (3) Not more than ten days in all other cases.
      In each instance the burden shall be on the landlord to see
that remedial work under this section is completed promptly. If
completion is delayed due to circumstances beyond the landlord's
control, including the unavailability of financing, the landlord
shall remedy the defective condition as soon as possible. [1989 c
342 § 4; 1973 1st ex.s. c 207 § 7.]

RCW 59.18.075 Seizure of illegal drugs--Notification of
landlord. (1) Any law enforcement agency which seizes a legend
drug pursuant to a violation of chapter 69.41 RCW, a controlled
substance pursuant to a violation of chapter 69.50 RCW, or an
imitation controlled substance pursuant to a violation of chapter
69.52 RCW, shall make a reasonable attempt to discover the identity
of the landlord and shall notify the landlord in writing, at the
last address listed in the property tax records and at any other
address known to the law enforcement agency, of the seizure and the
location of the seizure of the illegal drugs or substances.
      (2) Any law enforcement agency which arrests a tenant for
threatening another tenant with a firearm or other deadly weapon,
or for some other unlawful use of a firearm or other deadly weapon
on the rental premises, or for physically assaulting another person
on the rental premises, shall make a reasonable attempt to discover
the identity of the landlord and notify the landlord about the
arrest in writing, at the last address listed in the property tax
records and at any other address known to the law enforcement
agency. [1992 c 38 § 4; 1988 c 150 § 11.]

RCW 59.18.085 Rental of condemned or unlawful dwelling--
Tenant's remedies. (1) If a governmental agency responsible for
the enforcement of a building, housing, or other appropriate code
has notified the landlord that a dwelling is condemned or unlawful
to occupy due to the existence of conditions that violate
applicable codes, statutes, ordinances, or regulations, a landlord
shall not enter into a rental agreement for the dwelling unit until
the conditions are corrected.
      (2) If a landlord knowingly violates subsection (1) of this
section, the tenant shall recover either three months' periodic
rent or up to treble the actual damages sustained as a result of
the violation, whichever is greater, costs of suit, or arbitration
and reasonable attorneys' fees. If the tenant elects to terminate
the tenancy as a result of the conditions leading to the posting,
or if the appropriate governmental agency requires that the tenant
vacate the premises, the tenant also shall recover:
      (a) The entire amount of any deposit prepaid by the tenant;
and
      (b) All prepaid rent. [1989 c 342 § 13.]

96

RCW 59.18.090 Landlord's failure to remedy defective condition--Tenant's choice of actions. If, after receipt of written notice, and expiration of the applicable period of time, as provided in RCW 59.18.070, the landlord fails to remedy the defective condition within a reasonable time the tenant may:

(1) Terminate the rental agreement and quit the premises upon written notice to the landlord without further obligation under the rental agreement, in which case he shall be discharged from payment of rent for any period following the quitting date, and shall be entitled to a pro rata refund of any prepaid rent, and shall receive a full and specific statement of the basis for retaining any of the deposit together with any refund due in accordance with RCW 59.18.280;

(2) Bring an action in an appropriate court, or at arbitration if so agreed, for any remedy provided under this chapter or otherwise provided by law; or

(3) Pursue other remedies available under this chapter. [1973 1st ex.s. c 207 § 9.]

RCW 59.18.100 Landlord's failure to carry out duties--Repairs effected by tenant--Procedure--Deduction of cost from rent--Limitations. (1) If at any time during the tenancy, the landlord fails to carry out any of the duties imposed by RCW 59.18.060, and notice of the defect is given to the landlord pursuant to RCW 59.18.070, the tenant may submit to the landlord or his designated agent by certified mail or in person a good faith estimate by the tenant of the cost to perform the repairs necessary to correct the defective condition if the repair is to be done by licensed or registered persons, or if no licensing or registration requirement applies to the type of work to be performed, the cost if the repair is to be done by responsible persons capable of performing such repairs. Such estimate may be submitted to the landlord at the same time as notice is given pursuant to RCW 59.18.070: PROVIDED, That the remedy provided in this section shall not be available for a landlord's failure to carry out the duties in *RCW 59.18.060 (9), and (11): PROVIDED FURTHER, That if the tenant utilizes this section for repairs pursuant to RCW 59.18.060(6), the tenant shall promptly provide the landlord with a key to any new or replaced locks. The amount the tenant may deduct from the rent may vary from the estimate, but cannot exceed the one-month limit as described in subsection (2) of this section.

(2) If the landlord fails to commence remedial action of the defective condition within the applicable time period after receipt of notice and the estimate from the tenant, the tenant may contract with a licensed or registered person, or with a responsible person capable of performing the repair if no license or registration is required, to make the repair, and upon the completion of the repair and an opportunity for inspection by the landlord or his designated agent, the tenant may deduct the cost of repair from the rent in an amount not to exceed the sum expressed in dollars representing one month's rental of the tenant's unit per repair: PROVIDED, That when the landlord must commence to remedy the defective condition within ten days as provided in RCW 59.18.070(3), the tenant cannot contract for repairs for ten days after notice or five days after the landlord receives the estimate, whichever is later: PROVIDED FURTHER, That the total costs of repairs deducted in any twelve-month period under this subsection shall not exceed the sum expressed in dollars representing two month's rental of the tenant's unit.

(3) If the landlord fails to carry out the duties imposed by RCW 59.18.060 within the applicable time period, and if the cost of repair does not exceed one-half month's rent, including the cost of materials and labor, which shall be computed at the prevailing rate in the community for the performance of such work, and if repair of the condition need not by law be performed only by licensed or registered persons, and if the tenant has given notice under RCW 59.18.070, although no estimate shall be necessary under this subsection, the tenant may repair the defective condition in a workmanlike manner and upon completion of the repair and an opportunity for inspection, the tenant may deduct the cost of repair from the rent: PROVIDED, That repairs under this subsection are limited to defects within the leased premises: PROVIDED FURTHER, That the cost per repair shall not exceed one-half month's rent of the unit and that the total costs of repairs deducted in any twelve-month period under this subsection shall not exceed one month's rent of the unit.

(4) The provisions of this section shall not:

(a) Create a relationship of employer and employee between landlord and tenant; or

(b) Create liability under the workers' compensation act; or

(c) Constitute the tenant as an agent of the landlord for the purposes of **RCW 60.04.010 and 60.04.040.

(5) Any repair work performed under the provisions of this section shall comply with the requirements imposed by any applicable code, statute, ordinance, or regulation. A landlord whose property is damaged because of repairs performed in a negligent manner may recover the actual damages in an action against the tenant.

(6) Nothing in this section shall prevent the tenant from agreeing with the landlord to undertake the repairs himself in return for cash payment or a reasonable reduction in rent, the agreement thereof to be agreed upon between the parties, and such agreement does not alter the landlord's obligations under this chapter. [1989 c 342 § 5; 1987 c 185 § 35; 1973 1st ex.s. c 207 § 10.]

RCW 59.18.110 Failure of landlord to carry out duties--Determination by court or arbitrator--Judgment against landlord for diminished rental value and repair costs--Enforcement of judgment--Reduction in rent under certain conditions. (1) If a court or an arbitrator determines that:

(a) A landlord has failed to carry out a duty or duties imposed by RCW 59.18.060; and

(b) A reasonable time has passed for the landlord to remedy the defective condition following notice to the landlord in accordance with RCW 59.18.070 or such other time as may be allotted by the court or arbitrator; the court or arbitrator may determine the diminution in rental value of the premises due to the defective condition and shall render judgment against the landlord for the rent paid in excess of such diminished rental value from the time of notice of such defect to the time of decision and any costs of repair done pursuant to RCW 59.18.100 for which no deduction has been previously made. Such decisions may be enforced as other judgments at law and shall be available to the tenant as a set-off against any existing or subsequent claims of the landlord.

The court or arbitrator may also authorize the tenant to make or contract to make further corrective repairs: PROVIDED, That the court specifies a time period in which the landlord may make such repairs before the tenant may commence or contract for such repairs: PROVIDED FURTHER, That such repairs shall not exceed the sum expressed in dollars representing one month's rental of the tenant's unit in any one calendar year.

(2) The tenant shall not be obligated to pay rent in excess of the diminished rental value of the premises until such defect or defects are corrected by the landlord or until the court or arbitrator determines otherwise. [1973 1st ex.s. c 207 § 11.]

RCW 59.18.115 Substandard and dangerous conditions--Notice to landlord--Government certification--Escrow account. (1) The legislature finds that some tenants live in residences that are substandard and dangerous to their health and safety and that the repair and deduct remedies of RCW 59.18.100 may not be adequate to remedy substandard and dangerous conditions. Therefore, an extraordinary remedy is necessary if the conditions substantially endanger or impair the health and safety of the tenant.

(2)(a) If a landlord fails to fulfill any substantial obligation imposed by RCW 59.18.060 that substantially endangers or impairs the health or safety of a tenant, including (i) structural members that are of insufficient size or strength to carry imposed loads with safety, (ii) exposure of the occupants to the weather, (iii) plumbing and sanitation defects that directly expose the occupants to the risk of illness or injury, (iv) lack of water, including hot water, (v) heating or ventilation systems that are not functional or are hazardous, (vi) defective, hazardous, or missing electrical wiring or electrical service, (vii) defective or inadequate exits that increase the risk of injury to occupants, and (viii) conditions that increase the risk of fire, the tenant shall give notice in writing to the landlord, specifying the conditions, acts, omissions, or violations. Such notice shall be sent to the landlord or to the person or place where rent is normally paid.

(b) If after receipt of the notice described in (a) of this subsection the landlord fails to remedy the condition or conditions within a reasonable amount of time under RCW 59.18.070, the tenant may request that the local government provide for an inspection of the premises with regard to the specific condition or conditions that exist as provided in (a) of this subsection. The local government shall have the appropriate government official, or may designate a public or disinterested private person or company capable of conducting the inspection and making the certification, conduct an inspection of the specific condition or conditions listed by the tenant, and shall not inspect nor be liable for any other condition or conditions of the premises. The purpose of this inspection is to verify, to the best of the inspector's ability, whether the tenant's listed condition or conditions exist and substantially endanger the tenant's health or safety under (a) of this subsection; the inspection is for the purposes of this private civil remedy, and therefore shall not be related to any other governmental function such as enforcement of any code, ordinance, or state law.

(c) The local government or its designee, after receiving the request from the tenant to conduct an inspection under this section, shall conduct the inspection and make any certification within a reasonable amount of time not more than five days from the date of receipt of the request. The local government or its designee may enter the premises at any reasonable time to do the inspection, provided that he or she first shall display proper credentials and request entry. The local government or its designee shall whenever practicable, taking into consideration the imminence of any threat to the tenant's health or safety, give the landlord at least twenty-four hours notice of the date and time of inspection and provide the landlord with an opportunity to be present at the time of the inspection. The landlord shall have no power or authority to prohibit entry for the inspection.

(d) The local government or its designee shall certify whether the condition or the conditions specified by the tenant do exist and do make the premises substantially unfit for human habitation or can be a substantial risk to the health and safety of the tenant as described in (a) of this subsection. The certification shall be provided to the tenant, and a copy shall be included by the tenant with the notice sent to the landlord under subsection (3) of this section. The certification may be appealed to the local board of appeals, but the appeal shall not delay or preclude the tenant from proceeding with the escrow under this section.

(e) The tenant shall not be entitled to deposit rent in escrow pursuant to this section unless the tenant first makes a good faith determination that he or she is unable to repair the conditions described in the certification issued pursuant to subsection (2)(d) of this section through use of the repair remedies authorized by RCW 59.18.100.

(f) If the local government or its designee certifies that the condition or conditions specified by the tenant exist, the tenant shall then either pay the periodic rent due to the landlord or deposit all periodic rent then called for in the rental agreement and all rent thereafter called for in the rental agreement into an escrow account maintained by a person authorized by law to set up and maintain escrow accounts, including escrow companies under chapter 18.44 RCW, financial institutions, or attorneys, or with the clerk of the court of the district or superior court where the property is located. These depositories are hereinafter referred to as "escrow." The tenant shall notify the landlord in writing of the deposit by mailing the notice postage prepaid by first class mail or by delivering the notice to the landlord promptly but not more than twenty-four hours after the deposit.

(g) This section, when elected as a remedy by the tenant by sending the notice under subsection (3) of this section, shall be the exclusive remedy available to the tenant regarding defects described in the certification under subsection (2)(d) of this section: PROVIDED, That the tenant may simultaneously commence or pursue an action in an appropriate court, or at arbitration if so agreed, to determine past, present, or future diminution in rental value of the premises due to any defective conditions.

(3) The notice to the landlord of the rent escrow under this section shall be a sworn statement by the tenant in substantially the following form:

NOTICE TO LANDLORD OF RENT ESCROW

Name of tenant:
Name of landlord:
Name and address of escrow:
Date of deposit of rent into escrow:
Amount of rent deposited into escrow:
The following condition has been certified by a local building official to substantially endanger, impair, or affect the health or safety of a tenant:
That written notice of the conditions needing repair was provided to the landlord on . . ., and . . . days have elapsed and the repairs have not been made.

. . . .
        (Sworn Signature)

(4) The escrow shall place all rent deposited in a separate rent escrow account in the name of the escrow in a bank or savings and loan association domiciled in this state. The escrow shall keep in a separate docket an account of each deposit, with the name and address of the tenant, and the name and address of the landlord and of the agent, if any.

(5)(a) A landlord who receives notice that the rent due has been deposited with an escrow pursuant to subsection (2) of this section may:

(i) Apply to the escrow for release of the funds after the local government certifies that the repairs to the conditions listed in the notice under subsection (3) of this section have been properly repaired. The escrow shall release the funds to the landlord less any escrow costs for which the tenant is entitled to reimbursement pursuant to this section, immediately upon written receipt of the local government certification that the repairs to the conditions listed in the notice under subsection (3) of this section have been properly completed.

(ii) File an action with the court and apply to the court for release of the rent on the grounds that the tenant did not comply with the notice requirement of subsection (2) or (3) of this section. Proceedings under this subsection shall be governed by the time, service, and filing requirements of RCW 59.18.370 regarding show cause hearings.

(iii) File an action with the court and apply to the court for release of the rent on the grounds that there was no violation of any obligation imposed upon the landlord or that the condition has been remedied.

(iv) This action may be filed in any court having jurisdiction, including small claims court. If the tenant has vacated the premises or if the landlord has failed to commence an action with the court for release of the funds within sixty days after rent is deposited in escrow, the tenant may file an action to determine how and when any rent deposited in escrow shall be released or disbursed. The landlord shall not commence an unlawful detainer action for nonpayment of rent by serving or filing a summons and complaint if the tenant initially pays the rent called for in the rental agreement that is due into escrow as provided for under this section on or before the date rent is due or on or before the expiration of a three-day notice to pay rent or vacate and continues to pay the rent into escrow as the rent becomes due or prior to the expiration of a three-day notice to pay rent or vacate; provided that the landlord shall not be barred from commencing an unlawful detainer action for nonpayment of rent if the amount of rent that is paid into escrow is less than the amount of rent agreed upon in the rental agreement between the parties.

(b) The tenant shall be named as a party to any action filed by the landlord under this section, and shall have the right to file an answer and counterclaim, although any counterclaim shall be dismissed without prejudice if the court or arbitrator determines that the tenant failed to follow the notice requirements contained in this section. Any counterclaim can only claim diminished rental value related to conditions specified by the tenant in the notice required under subsection (3) of this section. This limitation on the tenant's right to counterclaim shall not affect the tenant's right to bring his or her own separate action. A trial shall be held within sixty days of the date of filing of the landlord's or tenant's complaint.

(c) The tenant shall be entitled to reimbursement for any escrow costs or fees incurred for setting up or maintaining an escrow account pursuant to this section, unless the tenant did not comply with the notice requirements of subsection (2) or (3) of this section. Any escrow fees that are incurred for which the tenant is entitled to reimbursement shall be deducted from the rent deposited in escrow and remitted to the tenant at such time as any rent is released to the landlord. The prevailing party in any court action or arbitration brought under this section may also be awarded its costs and reasonable attorneys' fees.

(d) If a court determines a diminished rental value of the premises, the tenant may pay the rent due based on the diminished value of the premises into escrow until the landlord makes the necessary repairs.

(6)(a) If a landlord brings an action for the release of rent deposited, the court may, upon application of the landlord, release part of the rent on deposit for payment of the debt service on the premises, the insurance premiums for the premises, utility services, and repairs to the rental unit.

(b) In determining whether to release rent for the payments described in (a) of this subsection, the court shall consider the amount of rent the landlord receives from other rental units in the buildings of which the residential premises are a part, the cost of operating those units, and the costs which may be required to remedy the condition contained in the notice. The court shall also consider whether the expenses are due or have already been paid, whether the landlord has other financial resources, or whether the landlord or tenant will suffer irreparable damage. The court may request the landlord to provide additional security, such as a bond, prior to authorizing release of any of the funds in escrow. [1989 c 342 § 16.]

RCW 59.18.120 Defective condition--Unfeasible to remedy defect--Termination of tenancy. If a court or arbitrator determines a defective condition as described in RCW 59.18.060 to be so substantial that it is unfeasible for the landlord to remedy the defect within the time allotted by RCW 59.18.070, and that the tenant should not remain in the dwelling unit in its defective condition, the court or arbitrator may authorize the termination of the tenancy: PROVIDED, That the court or arbitrator shall set a reasonable time for the tenant to vacate the premises. [1973 1st ex.s. c 207 § 12.]

RCW 59.18.130 Duties of tenant. Each tenant shall pay the rental amount at such times and in such amounts as provided for in the rental agreement or as otherwise provided by law and comply with all obligations imposed upon tenants by applicable provisions of all municipal, county, and state codes, statutes, ordinances, and regulations, and in addition shall:

(1) Keep that part of the premises which he or she occupies and uses as clean and sanitary as the conditions of the premises permit;

(2) Properly dispose from his or her dwelling unit all rubbish, garbage, and other organic or flammable waste, in a clean and sanitary manner at reasonable and regular intervals, and assume all costs of extermination and fumigation for infestation caused by the tenant;

(3) Properly use and operate all electrical, gas, heating, plumbing and other fixtures and appliances supplied by the landlord;

(4) Not intentionally or negligently destroy, deface, damage, impair, or remove any part of the structure or dwelling, with the appurtenances thereto, including the facilities, equipment, furniture, furnishings, and appliances, or permit any member of his or her family, invitee, licensee, or any person acting under his or her control to do so. Violations may be prosecuted under chapter 9A.48 RCW if the destruction is intentional and malicious;

(5) Not permit a nuisance or common waste;

(6) Not engage in drug-related activity at the rental premises, or allow a subtenant, sublessee, resident, or anyone else to engage in drug-related activity at the rental premises with the knowledge or consent of the tenant. "Drug-related activity" means that activity which constitutes a violation of chapter 69.41, 69.50, or 69.52 RCW;

(7) Maintain the smoke detection device in accordance with the manufacturer's recommendations, including the replacement of batteries where required for the proper operation of the smoke detection device, as required in RCW 48.48.140(3);

(8) Not engage in any activity at the rental premises that is:
(a) Imminently hazardous to the physical safety of other persons on the premises; and
(b)(i) Entails physical assaults upon another person which result in an arrest; or
(ii) Entails the unlawful use of a firearm or other deadly weapon as defined in RCW 9A.04.110 which results in an arrest, including threatening another tenant or the landlord with a firearm or other deadly weapon under RCW 59.18.352. Nothing in this subsection (8) shall authorize the termination of tenancy and eviction of the victim of a physical assault or the victim of the use or threatened use of a firearm or other deadly weapon;
(9) Not engage in any gang-related activity at the premises, as defined in RCW 59.18.030, or allow another to engage in such activity at the premises, that renders people in at least two or more dwelling units or residences insecure in life or the use of property or that injures or endangers the safety or health of people in at least two or more dwelling units or residences. In determining whether a tenant is engaged in gang-related activity, a court should consider the totality of the circumstances, including factors such as whether there have been a significant number of complaints to the landlord about the tenant's activities at the property, damages done by the tenant to the property, including the property of other tenants or neighbors, harassment or threats made by the tenant to other tenants or neighbors that have been reported to law enforcement agencies, any police incident reports involving the tenant, and the tenant's criminal history; and
(10) Upon termination and vacation, restore the premises to their initial condition except for reasonable wear and tear or conditions caused by failure of the landlord to comply with his or her obligations under this chapter: PROVIDED, That the tenant shall not be charged for normal cleaning if he or she has paid a nonrefundable cleaning fee. [1998 c 276 § 2; 1992 c 38 § 2; 1991 c 154 § 3; 1988 c 150 § 2; 1983 c 264 § 3; 1973 1st ex.s. c 207 § 13.]

RCW 59.18.140 Reasonable obligations or restrictions—Tenant's duty to conform. The tenant shall conform to all reasonable obligations or restrictions, whether denominated by the landlord as rules, rental agreement, rent, or otherwise, concerning the use, occupation, and maintenance of his dwelling unit, appurtenances thereto, and the property of which the dwelling unit is a part if such obligations and restrictions are not in violation of any of the terms of this chapter and are not otherwise contrary to law, and if such obligations and restrictions are brought to the attention of the tenant at the time of his initial occupancy of the dwelling unit and thus become part of the rental agreement. Except for termination of tenancy, after thirty days written notice to each affected tenant, a new rule of tenancy including a change in the amount of rent may become effective upon completion of the term of the rental agreement or sooner upon mutual consent. [1989 c 342 § 6; 1973 1st ex.s. c 207 § 14.]

RCW 59.18.150 Landlord's right of entry—Purposes—Conditions. (1) The tenant shall not unreasonably withhold consent to the landlord to enter into the dwelling unit in order to inspect the premises, make necessary or agreed repairs, alterations, or improvements, supply necessary or agreed services, or exhibit the dwelling unit to prospective or actual purchasers, mortgagees, tenants, workers, or contractors.

(2) The landlord may enter the dwelling unit without consent of the tenant in case of emergency or abandonment.

(3) The landlord shall not abuse the right of access or use it to harass the tenant. Except in the case of emergency or if it is impracticable to do so, the landlord shall give the tenant at least two days' notice of his or her intent to enter and shall enter only at reasonable times. The tenant shall not unreasonably withhold consent to the landlord to enter the dwelling unit at a specified time where the landlord has given at least one day's notice of intent to enter to exhibit the dwelling unit to prospective or actual purchasers or tenants. A landlord shall not unreasonably interfere with a tenant's enjoyment of the rented dwelling unit by excessively exhibiting the dwelling unit.

(4) The landlord has no other right of access except by court order, arbitrator or by consent of the tenant.

(5) A landlord or tenant who continues to violate this section after being served with one written notification alleging in good faith violations of this section listing the date and time of the violation shall be liable for up to one hundred dollars for each violation after receipt of the notice. The prevailing party may recover costs of the suit or arbitration under this section, and may also recover reasonable attorneys' fees. [1989 c 342 § 7; 1989 c 12 § 18; 1973 1st ex.s. c 207 § 15.]

RCW 59.18.160 Landlord's remedies if tenant fails to remedy defective condition. If, after receipt of written notice, as provided in RCW 59.18.170, the tenant fails to remedy the defective condition within a reasonable time, the landlord may:

(1) Bring an action in an appropriate court, or at arbitration if so agreed for any remedy provided under this chapter or otherwise provided by law; or

(2) Pursue other remedies available under this chapter. [1973 1st ex.s. c 207 § 16.]

RCW 59.18.170 Landlord to give notice if tenant fails to carry out duties. If at any time during the tenancy the tenant fails to carry out the duties required by RCW 59.18.130 or 59.18.140, the landlord may, in addition to pursuit of remedies otherwise provided by law, give written notice to the tenant of said failure, which notice shall specify the nature of the failure. [1973 1st ex.s. c 207 § 17.]

RCW 59.18.180 Tenant's failure to comply with statutory duties--Landlord to give tenant written notice of noncompliance--Landlord's remedies. (1) If the tenant fails to comply with any portion of RCW 59.18.130 or 59.18.140, and such noncompliance can substantially affect the health and safety of the tenant or other tenants, or substantially increase the hazards of fire or accident that can be remedied by repair, replacement of a damaged item, or cleaning, the tenant shall comply within thirty days after written notice by the landlord specifying the noncompliance, or, in the case of emergency as promptly as conditions require. If the tenant fails to remedy the noncompliance within that period the landlord may enter the dwelling unit and cause the work to be done and submit an itemized bill of the actual and reasonable cost of repair, to be payable on the next date when periodic rent is due, or on terms mutually agreed to by the landlord and tenant, or immediately if the rental agreement has terminated. Any substantial noncompliance by the tenant of RCW 59.18.130 or 59.18.140 shall constitute a ground for commencing an action in unlawful detainer in accordance with the provisions of chapter 59.12 RCW, and a landlord may commence such action at any time after written notice pursuant to such chapter. The tenant shall have a defense to an unlawful detainer action filed solely on this ground if it is determined at the hearing authorized under the provisions of chapter 59.12 RCW that the tenant is in substantial compliance with the provisions of this section, or if the tenant remedies the noncomplying condition within the thirty day period provided for above or any shorter period determined at the hearing to have been required because of an emergency: PROVIDED, That if the defective condition is remedied after the commencement of an unlawful detainer action, the tenant may be liable to the landlord for statutory costs and reasonable attorney's fees.

(2) If drug-related activity is alleged to be a basis for termination of tenancy under RCW 59.18.130(6), 59.12.030(5), or 59.20.140(5), the compliance provisions of this section do not apply and the landlord may proceed directly to an unlawful detainer action.

(3) If activity on the premises that creates an imminent hazard to the physical safety of other persons on the premises as defined in RCW 59.18.130(8) is alleged to be the basis for termination of the tenancy, and the tenant is arrested as a result of this activity, then the compliance provisions of this section do not apply and the landlord may proceed directly to an unlawful detainer action against the tenant who was arrested for this activity.

(4) If gang-related activity, as prohibited under RCW 59.18.130(9), is alleged to be the basis for termination of the tenancy, then the compliance provisions of this section do not apply and the landlord may proceed directly to an unlawful detainer action in accordance with chapter 59.12 RCW, and a landlord may commence such an action at any time after written notice under chapter 59.12 RCW.

(5) A landlord may not be held liable in any cause of action for bringing an unlawful detainer action against a tenant for drug-related activity, for creating an imminent hazard to the physical safety of others, or for engaging in gang-related activity that renders people in at least two or more dwelling units or residences insecure in life or the use of property or that injures or endangers the safety or health of people in at least two or more dwelling units or residences under this section, if the unlawful detainer action was brought in good faith. Nothing in this section shall affect a landlord's liability under RCW 59.18.380 to pay all damages sustained by the tenant should the writ of restitution be wrongfully sued out. [1998 c 276 § 3; 1992 c 38 § 3; 1988 c 150 § 7; 1973 1st ex.s. c 207 § 18.]

RCW 59.18.190 Notice to tenant to remedy nonconformance.
Whenever the landlord learns of a breach of RCW 59.18.130 or has
accepted performance by the tenant which is at variance with the
terms of the rental agreement or rules enforceable after the
commencement of the tenancy, he may immediately give notice to the
tenant to remedy the nonconformance. Said notice shall expire
after sixty days unless the landlord pursues any remedy under this
chapter. [1973 1st ex.s. c 207 § 19.]

RCW 59.18.200 Tenancy from month to month or for rental
period--Termination--Exclusion of children or conversion to
condominium--Notice. (1) When premises are rented for an
indefinite time, with monthly or other periodic rent reserved, such
tenancy shall be construed to be a tenancy from month to month, or
from period to period on which rent is payable, and shall be
terminated by written notice of twenty days or more, preceding the
end of any of said months or periods, given by either party to the
other.
    (2) Whenever a landlord plans to change any apartment or
apartments to a condominium form of ownership or plans to change to
a policy of excluding children, the landlord shall give a written
notice to a tenant at least ninety days before termination of the
tenancy to effectuate such change in policy. Such ninety-day
notice shall be in lieu of the notice required by subsection (1) of
this section: PROVIDED, That if after giving the ninety-day notice
the change in policy is delayed, the notice requirements of
subsection (1) of this section shall apply unless waived by the
tenant. [1979 ex.s. c 70 § 1; 1973 1st ex.s. c 207 § 20.]

RCW 59.18.210 Tenancies from year to year except under
written contract. Tenancies from year to year are hereby abolished
except when the same are created by express written contract.
Leases may be in writing or print, or partly in writing and partly
in print, and shall be legal and valid for any term or period not
exceeding one year, without acknowledgment, witnesses or seals.
[1973 1st ex.s. c 207 § 21.]

RCW 59.18.220 Termination of tenancy for a specified time.
In all cases where premises are rented for a specified time, by
express or implied contract, the tenancy shall be deemed terminated
at the end of such specified time. [1973 1st ex.s. c 207 § 22.]

RCW 59.18.230 Waiver of chapter provisions prohibited--
Provisions prohibited from rental agreement--Distress for rent
abolished--Detention of personal property for rent--Remedies. (1)
Any provision of a lease or other agreement, whether oral or
written, whereby any section or subsection of this chapter is
waived except as provided in RCW 59.18.360 and shall be deemed
against public policy and shall be unenforceable. Such
unenforceability shall not affect other provisions of the agreement
which can be given effect without them.

(2) No rental agreement may provide that the tenant:
(a) Agrees to waive or to forego rights or remedies under this chapter; or
(b) Authorizes any person to confess judgment on a claim arising out of the rental agreement; or
(c) Agrees to pay the landlord's attorney's fees, except as authorized in this chapter; or
(d) Agrees to the exculpation or limitation of any liability of the landlord arising under law or to indemnify the landlord for that liability or the costs connected therewith; or
(e) And landlord have agreed to a particular arbitrator at the time the rental agreement is entered into.
(3) A provision prohibited by subsection (2) of this section included in a rental agreement is unenforceable. If a landlord deliberately uses a rental agreement containing provisions known by him to be prohibited, the tenant may recover actual damages sustained by him and reasonable attorney's fees.
(4) The common law right of the landlord of distress for rent is hereby abolished for property covered by this chapter. Any provision in a rental agreement creating a lien upon the personal property of the tenant or authorizing a distress for rent is null and void and of no force and effect. Any landlord who takes or detains the personal property of a tenant without the specific written consent of the tenant to such incident of taking or detention, and who, after written demand by the tenant for the return of his personal property, refuses to return the same promptly shall be liable to the tenant for the value of the property retained, actual damages, and if the refusal is intentional, may also be liable for damages of up to one hundred dollars per day but not to exceed one thousand dollars, for each day or part of a day that the tenant is deprived of his property. The prevailing party may recover his costs of suit and a reasonable attorney's fee.
In any action, including actions pursuant to chapters 7.64 or 12.28 RCW, brought by a tenant or other person to recover possession of his personal property taken or detained by a landlord in violation of this section, the court, upon motion and after notice to the opposing parties, may waive or reduce any bond requirements where it appears to be to the satisfaction of the court that the moving party is proceeding in good faith and has, prima facie, a meritorious claim for immediate delivery or redelivery of said property. [1989 c 342 § 8; 1983 c 264 § 4; 1973 1st ex.s. c 207 § 23.]

RCW 59.18.240 Reprisals or retaliatory actions by landlord--Prohibited. So long as the tenant is in compliance with this chapter, the landlord shall not take or threaten to take reprisals or retaliatory action against the tenant because of any good faith and lawful:
(1) Complaints or reports by the tenant to a governmental authority concerning the failure of the landlord to substantially comply with any code, statute, ordinance, or regulation governing the maintenance or operation of the premises, if such condition may endanger or impair the health or safety of the tenant; or

(2) Assertions or enforcement by the tenant of his rights and remedies under this chapter.

"Reprisal or retaliatory action" shall mean and include but not be limited to any of the following actions by the landlord when such actions are intended primarily to retaliate against a tenant because of the tenant's good faith and lawful act:

(a) Eviction of the tenant;
(b) Increasing the rent required of the tenant;
(c) Reduction of services to the tenant; and
(d) Increasing the obligations of the tenant. [1983 c 264 § 9; 1973 1st ex.s. c 207 § 24.]

RCW 59.18.250 Reprisals or retaliatory actions by landlord-- Presumptions--Rebuttal--Costs. Initiation by the landlord of any action listed in RCW 59.18.240 within ninety days after a good faith and lawful act by the tenant as enumerated in RCW 59.18.240, or within ninety days after any inspection or proceeding of a governmental agency resulting from such act, shall create a rebuttable presumption affecting the burden of proof, that the action is a reprisal or retaliatory action against the tenant: PROVIDED, That if at the time the landlord gives notice of termination of tenancy pursuant to chapter 59.12 RCW the tenant is in arrears in rent or in breach of any other lease or rental obligation, there is a rebuttable presumption affecting the burden of proof that the landlord's action is neither a reprisal nor retaliatory action against the tenant: PROVIDED FURTHER, That if the court finds that the tenant made a complaint or report to a governmental authority within ninety days after notice of a proposed increase in rent or other action in good faith by the landlord, there is a rebuttable presumption that the complaint or report was not made in good faith: PROVIDED FURTHER, That no presumption against the landlord shall arise under this section, with respect to an increase in rent, if the landlord, in a notice to the tenant of increase in rent, specifies reasonable grounds for said increase, which grounds may include a substantial increase in market value due to remedial action under this chapter: PROVIDED FURTHER, That the presumption of retaliation, with respect to an eviction, may be rebutted by evidence that it is not practical to make necessary repairs while the tenant remains in occupancy. In any action or eviction proceeding where the tenant prevails upon his claim or defense that the landlord has violated this section, the tenant shall be entitled to recover his costs of suit or arbitration, including a reasonable attorney's fee, and where the landlord prevails upon his claim he shall be entitled to recover his costs of suit or arbitration, including a reasonable attorney's fee: PROVIDED FURTHER, That neither party may recover attorney's fees to the extent that their legal services are provided at no cost to them. [1983 c 264 § 10; 1973 1st ex.s. c 207 § 25.]

RCW 59.18.253 Deposit to secure occupancy by tenant-- Landlord's duties--Violation. (1) It shall be unlawful for a landlord to require a fee from a prospective tenant for the privilege of being placed on a waiting list to be considered as a tenant for a dwelling unit.

(2) A landlord who charges a prospective tenant a fee or deposit to secure that the prospective tenant will move into a dwelling unit, after the dwelling unit has been offered to the prospective tenant, must provide the prospective tenant with a receipt for the fee or deposit, together with a written statement of the conditions, if any, under which the fee or deposit is refundable. If the prospective tenant does occupy the dwelling unit, then the landlord must credit the amount of the fee or deposit to the tenant's first month's rent or to the tenant's security deposit. If the prospective tenant does not occupy the dwelling unit, then the landlord may keep up to the full amount of any fee or deposit that was paid by the prospective tenant to secure the tenancy, so long as it is in accordance with the written statement of conditions furnished to the prospective tenant at the time the fee or deposit was charged. A fee charged to secure a tenancy under this subsection does not include any cost charged by a landlord to use a tenant screening service or obtain background information on a prospective tenant.

(3) In any action brought for a violation of this section a landlord may be liable for the amount of the fee or deposit charged. In addition, any landlord who violates this section may be liable to the prospective tenant for an amount not to exceed one hundred dollars. The prevailing party may also recover court costs and a reasonable attorneys' fee. [1991 c 194 § 2.]

RCW 59.18.257 Screening of tenants--Costs--Notice to tenant--Violation. (1) If a landlord uses a tenant screening service, then the landlord may only charge for the costs incurred for using the tenant screening service under this section. If a landlord conducts his or her own screening of tenants, then the landlord may charge his or her actual costs in obtaining the background information, but the amount may not exceed the customary costs charged by a screening service in the general area. The landlord's actual costs include costs incurred for long distance phone calls and for time spent calling landlords, employers, and financial institutions.
(2) A landlord may not charge a prospective tenant for the cost of obtaining background information under this section unless the landlord first notifies the prospective tenant in writing of what a tenant screening entails, the prospective tenant's rights to dispute the accuracy of information provided by the tenant screening service or provided by the entities listed on the tenant application who will be contacted for information concerning the tenant, and the name and address of the tenant screening service used by the landlord.
(3) Nothing in this section requires a landlord to disclose information to a prospective tenant that was obtained from a tenant screening service or from entities listed on the tenant application which is not required under the federal fair credit reporting act, 15 U.S.C. Sec. 1681 et seq.
(4) Any landlord who violates this section may be liable to the prospective tenant for an amount not to exceed one hundred dollars. The prevailing party may also recover court costs and reasonable attorneys' fees. [1991 c 194 § 3.]

RCW 59.18.260 Moneys paid as deposit or security for performance by tenant--Written rental agreement to specify terms and conditions for retention by landlord--Written checklist required. If any moneys are paid to the landlord by the tenant as a deposit or as security for performance of the tenant's obligations in a lease or rental agreement, the lease or rental agreement shall be in writing and shall include the terms and conditions under which the deposit or portion thereof may be withheld by the landlord upon termination of the lease or rental agreement. If all or part of the deposit may be withheld to indemnify the landlord for damages to the premises for which the tenant is responsible, the rental agreement shall be in writing and shall so specify. No deposit may be collected by a landlord unless the rental agreement is in writing and a written checklist or statement specifically describing the condition and cleanliness of or existing damages to the premises and furnishings, including, but not limited to, walls, floors, countertops, carpets, drapes, furniture, and appliances, is provided by the landlord to the tenant at the commencement of the tenancy. The checklist or statement shall be signed and dated by the landlord and the tenant, and the tenant shall be provided with a copy of the signed checklist or statement. No such deposit shall be withheld on account of normal wear and tear resulting from ordinary use of the premises. [1983 c 264 § 6; 1973 1st ex.s. c 207 § 26.]

RCW 59.18.270 Moneys paid as deposit or security for performance by tenant--Deposit by landlord in trust account--Receipt--Claims. All moneys paid to the landlord by the tenant as a deposit as security for performance of the tenant's obligations in a lease or rental agreement shall promptly be deposited by the landlord in a trust account, maintained by the landlord for the purpose of holding such security deposits for tenants of the landlord, in a bank, savings and loan association, mutual savings bank, or licensed escrow agent located in Washington. Unless otherwise agreed in writing, the landlord shall be entitled to receipt of interest paid on such trust account deposits. The landlord shall provide the tenant with a written receipt for the deposit and shall provide written notice of the name and address and location of the depository and any subsequent change thereof. If during a tenancy the status of landlord is transferred to another, any sums in the deposit trust account affected by such transfer shall simultaneously be transferred to an equivalent trust account of the successor landlord, and the successor landlord shall promptly notify the tenant of the transfer and of the name, address and location of the new depository. The tenant's claim to any moneys paid under this section shall be prior to that of any creditor of the landlord, including a trustee in bankruptcy or receiver, even if such moneys are commingled. [1975 1st ex.s. c 233 § 1; 1973 1st ex.s. c 207 § 27.]

RCW 59.18.280 Moneys paid as deposit or security for performance by tenant--Statement and notice of basis for retention--Remedies for landlord's failure to make refund. Within fourteen days after the termination of the rental agreement and vacation of the premises or, if the tenant abandons the premises as defined in RCW 59.18.310, within fourteen days after the landlord learns of the abandonment, the landlord shall give a full and specific statement of the basis for retaining any of the deposit together with the payment of any refund due the tenant under the terms and conditions of the rental agreement. No portion of any deposit shall be withheld on account of wear resulting from ordinary use of the premises. The landlord complies with this section if the required statement or payment, or both, are deposited in the United States mail properly addressed with first class postage prepaid within the fourteen days.

The notice shall be delivered to the tenant personally or by mail to his last known address. If the landlord fails to give such statement together with any refund due the tenant within the time limits specified above he shall be liable to the tenant for the full amount of the deposit. The landlord is also barred in any action brought by the tenant to recover the deposit from asserting any claim or raising any defense for retaining any of the deposit unless the landlord shows that circumstances beyond the landlord's control prevented the landlord from providing the statement within the fourteen days or that the tenant abandoned the premises as defined in RCW 59.18.310. The court may in its discretion award up to two times the amount of the deposit for the intentional refusal of the landlord to give the statement or refund due. In any action brought by the tenant to recover the deposit, the prevailing party shall additionally be entitled to the cost of suit or arbitration including a reasonable attorney's fee.

Nothing in this chapter shall preclude the landlord from proceeding against, and the landlord shall have the right to proceed against a tenant to recover sums exceeding the amount of the tenant's damage or security deposit for damage to the property for which the tenant is responsible together with reasonable attorney's fees. [1989 c 342 § 9; 1983 c 264 § 7; 1973 1st ex.s. c 207 § 28.]

RCW 59.18.285 Nonrefundable fees not to be designated as deposit--Written rental agreement required. No moneys paid to the landlord which are nonrefundable may be designated as a deposit or as part of any deposit. If any moneys are paid to the landlord as a nonrefundable fee, the rental agreement shall be in writing and shall clearly specify that the fee is nonrefundable. [1983 c 264 § 5.]

RCW 59.18.290 Removal or exclusion of tenant from premises--Holding over or excluding landlord from premises after termination date. (1) It shall be unlawful for the landlord to remove or exclude from the premises the tenant thereof except under a court order so authorizing. Any tenant so removed or excluded in violation of this section may recover possession of the property or terminate the rental agreement and, in either case, may recover the actual damages sustained. The prevailing party may recover the costs of suit or arbitration and reasonable attorney's fees.

(2) It shall be unlawful for the tenant to hold over in the premises or exclude the landlord therefrom after the termination of the rental agreement except under a valid court order so authorizing. Any landlord so deprived of possession of premises in violation of this section may recover possession of the property and damages sustained by him, and the prevailing party may recover his costs of suit or arbitration and reasonable attorney's fees. [1973 1st ex.s. c 207 § 29.]

RCW 59.18.300 Termination of tenant's utility services--Tenant causing loss of landlord provided utility services. It shall be unlawful for a landlord to intentionally cause termination of any of his tenant's utility services, including water, heat, electricity, or gas, except for an interruption of utility services for a reasonable time in order to make necessary repairs. Any landlord who violates this section may be liable to such tenant for his actual damages sustained by him, and up to one hundred dollars for each day or part thereof the tenant is thereby deprived of any utility service, and the prevailing party may recover his costs of suit or arbitration and a reasonable attorney's fee. It shall be unlawful for a tenant to intentionally cause the loss of utility services provided by the landlord, including water, heat, electricity or gas, excepting as resulting from the normal occupancy of the premises. [1973 1st ex.s. c 207 § 30.]

RCW 59.18.310 Default in rent--Abandonment--Liability of tenant--Landlord's remedies--Sale of tenant's property by landlord. If the tenant defaults in the payment of rent and reasonably indicates by words or actions the intention not to resume tenancy, the tenant shall be liable for the following for such abandonment: PROVIDED, That upon learning of such abandonment of the premises the landlord shall make a reasonable effort to mitigate the damages resulting from such abandonment:
(1) When the tenancy is month-to-month, the tenant shall be liable for the rent for the thirty days following either the date the landlord learns of the abandonment, or the date the next regular rental payment would have become due, whichever first occurs.
(2) When the tenancy is for a term greater than month-to-month, the tenant shall be liable for the lesser of the following:
(a) The entire rent due for the remainder of the term; or
(b) All rent accrued during the period reasonably necessary to rerent the premises at a fair rental, plus the difference between such fair rental and the rent agreed to in the prior agreement, plus actual costs incurred by the landlord in rerenting the premises together with statutory court costs and reasonable attorney's fees.

In the event of such abandonment of tenancy and an accompanying default in the payment of rent by the tenant, the landlord may immediately enter and take possession of any property of the tenant found on the premises and may store the same in any reasonably secure place. A landlord shall make reasonable efforts to provide the tenant with a notice containing the name and address of the landlord and the place where the property is stored and informing the tenant that a sale or disposition of the property shall take place pursuant to this section, and the date of the sale or disposal, and further informing the tenant of the right under RCW 59.18.230 to have the property returned prior to its sale or disposal. The landlord's efforts at notice under this subsection shall be satisfied by the mailing by first class mail, postage prepaid, of such notice to the tenant's last known address and to any other address provided in writing by the tenant or actually known to the landlord where the tenant might receive the notice. The landlord shall return the property to the tenant after the tenant has paid the actual or reasonable drayage and storage costs whichever is less if the tenant makes a written request for the return of the property before the landlord has sold or disposed of the property. After forty-five days from the date the notice of such sale or disposal is mailed or personally delivered to the tenant, the landlord may sell or dispose of such property, including personal papers, family pictures, and keepsakes. The landlord may apply any income derived therefrom against moneys due the landlord, including actual or reasonable costs whichever is less of drayage and storage of the property. If the property has a cumulative value of fifty dollars or less, the landlord may sell or dispose of the property in the manner provided in this section, except for personal papers, family pictures, and keepsakes, after seven days from the date the notice of sale or disposal is mailed or personally delivered to the tenant: PROVIDED, That the landlord shall make reasonable efforts, as defined in this section, to notify the tenant. Any excess income derived from the sale of such property under this section shall be held by the landlord for the benefit of the tenant for a period of one year from the date of sale, and if no claim is made or action commenced by the tenant for the recovery thereof prior to the expiration of that period of time, the balance shall be the property of the landlord, including any interest paid on the income. [1991 c 220 § 1; 1989 c 342 § 10; 1983 c 264 § 8; 1973 1st ex.s. c 207 § 31.]

RCW 59.18.315 Mediation of disputes by independent third party. The landlord and tenant may agree in writing to submit any dispute arising under the provisions of this chapter or under the terms, conditions, or performance of the rental agreement, to mediation by an independent third party. The parties may agree to submit any dispute to mediation before exercising their right to arbitration under RCW 59.18.320. [1983 c 264 § 11.]

RCW 59.18.320 Arbitration--Authorized--Exceptions--Notice-- Procedure. (1) The landlord and tenant may agree, in writing, except as provided in RCW 59.18.230(2)(e), to submit to arbitration, in conformity with the provisions of this section, any controversy arising under the provisions of this chapter, except the following:

(a) Controversies regarding the existence of defects covered in subsections (1) and (2) of RCW 59.18.070: PROVIDED, That this exception shall apply only before the implementation of any remedy by the tenant;

(b) Any situation where court action has been started by either landlord or tenant to enforce rights under this chapter; when the court action substantially affects the controversy, including but not limited to:

(i) Court action pursuant to subsections (2) and (3) of RCW 59.18.090 and subsections (1) and (2) of RCW 59.18.160; and

(ii) Any unlawful detainer action filed by the landlord pursuant to chapter 59.12 RCW.

(2) The party initiating arbitration under subsection (1) of this section shall give reasonable notice to the other party or parties.

(3) Except as otherwise provided in this section, the arbitration process shall be administered by any arbitrator agreed upon by the parties at the time the dispute arises: PROVIDED, That the procedures shall comply with the requirements of chapter 7.04 RCW (relating to arbitration) and of this chapter. [1973 1st ex.s. c 207 § 32.]

RCW 59.18.330 Arbitration--Application--Hearings--Decisions. (1) Unless otherwise mutually agreed to, in the event a controversy arises under RCW 59.18.320 the landlord or tenant, or both, shall complete an application for arbitration and deliver it to the selected arbitrator.

(2) The arbitrator so designated shall schedule a hearing to be held no later than ten days following receipt of notice of the controversy, except as provided in RCW 59.18.350.

(3) The arbitrator shall conduct public or private hearings. Reasonable notice of such hearings shall be given to the parties, who shall appear and be heard either in person or by counsel or other representative. Hearings shall be informal and the rules of evidence prevailing in judicial proceedings shall not be binding. A recording of the proceedings may be taken. Any oral or documentary evidence and other data deemed relevant by the arbitrator may be received in evidence. The arbitrator shall have the power to administer oaths, to issue subpoenas, to require the attendance of witnesses and the production of such books, papers, contracts, agreements, and documents as may be deemed by the arbitrator material to a just determination of the issues in dispute. If any person refuses to obey such subpoena or refuses to be sworn to testify, or any witness, party, or attorney is guilty of any contempt while in attendance at any hearing held hereunder, the arbitrator may invoke the jurisdiction of any superior court, and such court shall have jurisdiction to issue an appropriate order. A failure to obey such order may be punished by the court as a contempt thereof.

(4) Within five days after conclusion of the hearing, the arbitrator shall make a written decision upon the issues presented, a copy of which shall be mailed by certified mail or otherwise delivered to the parties or their designated representatives. The determination of the dispute made by the arbitrator shall be final and binding upon both parties.

(5) If a defective condition exists which affects more than one dwelling unit in a similar manner, the arbitrator may consolidate the issues of fact common to those dwelling units in a single proceeding.

(6) Decisions of the arbitrator shall be enforced or appealed according to the provisions of chapter 7.04 RCW. [1973 1st ex.s. c 207 § 33.]

RCW 59.18.340 Arbitration--Fee. The administrative fee for this arbitration procedure shall be established by agreement of the parties and the arbitrator and, unless otherwise allocated by the arbitrator, shall be shared equally by the parties: PROVIDED, That upon either party signing an affidavit to the effect that he is unable to pay his share of the fee, that portion of the fee may be waived or deferred. [1983 c 264 § 12; 1973 1st ex.s. c 207 § 34.]

RCW 59.18.350 Arbitration--Completion of arbitration after giving notice. When a party gives notice pursuant to subsection (2) of RCW 59.18.320, he must, at the same time, arrange for arbitration of the grievance in the manner provided for in this chapter. The arbitration shall be completed before the rental due date next occurring after the giving of notice pursuant to RCW 59.18.320: PROVIDED, That in no event shall the arbitrator have less than ten days to complete the arbitration process. [1973 1st ex.s. c 207 § 35.]

RCW 59.18.352 Threatening behavior by tenant--Termination of agreement--Written notice--Financial obligations. If a tenant notifies the landlord that he or she, or another tenant who shares that particular dwelling unit has been threatened by another tenant, and:
(1) The threat was made with a firearm or other deadly weapon as defined in RCW 9A.04.110; and
(2) The tenant who made the threat is arrested as a result of the threatening behavior; and
(3) The landlord fails to file an unlawful detainer action against the tenant who threatened another tenant within seven calendar days after receiving notice of the arrest from a law enforcement agency;
then the tenant who was threatened may terminate the rental agreement and quit the premises upon written notice to the landlord without further obligation under the rental agreement.
A tenant who terminates a rental agreement under this section is discharged from payment of rent for any period following the quitting date, and is entitled to a pro rata refund of any prepaid rent, and shall receive a full and specific statement of the basis for retaining any of the deposit together with any refund due in accordance with RCW 59.18.280.
Nothing in this section shall be construed to require a landlord to terminate a rental agreement or file an unlawful detainer action. [1992 c 38 § 5.]

RCW 59.18.354 Threatening behavior by landlord--Termination of agreement--Financial obligations. If a tenant is threatened by the landlord with a firearm or other deadly weapon as defined in RCW 9A.04.110, and the threat leads to an arrest of the landlord, then the tenant may terminate the rental agreement and quit the premises without further obligation under the rental agreement. The tenant is discharged from payment of rent for any period following the quitting date, and is entitled to a pro rata refund of any prepaid rent, and shall receive a full and specific statement of the basis for retaining any of the deposit together with any refund due in accordance with RCW 59.18.280. [1992 c 38 § 6.]

RCW 59.18.356 Threatening behavior--Violation of order for protection--Termination of agreement--Financial obligations. If a tenant notifies the landlord in writing that:

(1) He or she has a valid order for protection under chapter 26.50 RCW; and

(2) The person to be restrained has violated the order since the tenant occupied the dwelling unit; and

(3) The tenant has notified the sheriff of the county or the peace officers of the municipality in which the tenant resides of the violation; and

(4) A copy of the order for protection is available for the landlord;

then the tenant may terminate the rental agreement and quit the premises without further obligation under the rental agreement. A tenant who terminates a rental agreement under this section is discharged from the payment of rent for any period following the quitting date, and is entitled to a pro rata refund of any prepaid rent, and shall receive a full and specific statement of the basis for retaining any of the deposit together with any refund due in accordance with RCW 59.18.280.
[1992 c 38 § 7.]

RCW 59.18.360 Exemptions. A landlord and tenant may agree, in writing, to exempt themselves from the provisions of RCW 59.18.060, 59.18.100, 59.18.110, 59.18.120, 59.18.130, and 59.18.190 if the following conditions have been met:

(1) The agreement may not appear in a standard form lease or rental agreement;

(2) There is no substantial inequality in the bargaining position of the two parties;

(3) The exemption does not violate the public policy of this state in favor of the ensuring safe, and sanitary housing; and

(4) Either the local county prosecutor's office or the consumer protection division of the attorney general's office or the attorney for the tenant has approved in writing the application for exemption as complying with subsections (1) through (3) of this section. [1973 1st ex.s. c 207 § 36.]

RCW 59.18.365 Unlawful detainer action--Summons--Form. The summons for unlawful detainer actions for tenancies covered by this chapter shall be substantially in the following form. In unlawful detainer actions based on nonpayment of rent, the summons may contain the provisions authorized by RCW 59.18.375.

116

```
                IN THE SUPERIOR COURT OF THE STATE OF
                WASHINGTON IN AND FOR . . . . . . COUNTY

                                            *
            Plaintiff,                      *       NO.
                                            *
                vs.                         *       EVICTION SUMMONS
                                            *       (Residential)
            Defendant.                      *
                                            *
```

              THIS IS NOTICE OF A LAWSUIT TO EVICT YOU.
                    PLEASE READ IT CAREFULLY.
                  THE DEADLINE FOR YOUR WRITTEN
                          RESPONSE IS:
                   5:00 p.m., on . . . .

TO: . . . .   (Name)
       . . . .   (Address)

        This is notice of a lawsuit to evict you from the property
which you are renting. Your landlord is asking the court to
terminate your tenancy, direct the sheriff to remove you and your
belongings from the property, enter a money judgment against you
for unpaid rent and/or damages for your use of the property, and
for court costs and attorneys' fees.
        If you want to defend yourself in this lawsuit, you must
respond to the eviction complaint in writing on or before the
deadline stated above. You must respond in writing even if no case
number has been assigned by the court yet.
        You can respond to the complaint in writing by delivering a
copy of a notice of appearance or answer to your landlord's
attorney (or your landlord if there is no attorney) to be received
no later than the deadline stated above.
        The notice of appearance or answer must include the name of
this case (plaintiff(s) and defendant(s)), your name, the street
address where further legal papers may be sent, your telephone
number (if any), and your signature.
        If there is a number on the upper right side of the eviction
summons and complaint, you must also file your original notice of
appearance or answer with the court clerk by the deadline for your
written response.
        You may demand that the plaintiff file this lawsuit with the
court. If you do so, the demand must be in writing and must be
served upon the person signing the summons. Within fourteen days
after you serve the demand, the plaintiff must file this lawsuit
with the court, or the service on you of this summons and complaint
will be void.
        If you wish to seek the advice of an attorney in this matter,
you should do so promptly so that your written response, if any,
may be served on time.
        You may also be instructed in a separate order to appear for
a court hearing on your eviction. If you receive an order to show
cause you must personally appear at the hearing on the date
indicated in the order to show cause in addition to delivering and

filing your notice of appearance or answer by the deadline stated
above.

IF YOU DO NOT RESPOND TO THE COMPLAINT IN WRITING BY THE
DEADLINE STATED ABOVE YOU WILL LOSE BY DEFAULT. YOUR
LANDLORD MAY PROCEED WITH THE LAWSUIT, EVEN IF YOU HAVE
MOVED OUT OF THE PROPERTY.

The notice of appearance or answer must be delivered to:

. . . .

Name

. . . .

Address

. . . .

Telephone Number

[1989 c 342 § 15.]

RCW 59.18.370 Forcible entry or detainer or unlawful detainer
actions--Writ of restitution--Application--Order--Hearing. The
plaintiff, at the time of commencing an action of forcible entry or
detainer or unlawful detainer, or at any time afterwards, upon
filing the complaint, may apply to the superior court in which the
action is pending for an order directing the defendant to appear
and show cause, if any he has, why a writ of restitution should not
issue restoring to the plaintiff possession of the property in the
complaint described, and the judge shall by order fix a time and
place for a hearing of said motion, which shall not be less than
six nor more than twelve days from the date of service of said
order upon defendant. A copy of said order, together with a copy
of the summons and complaint if not previously served upon the
defendant, shall be served upon the defendant. Said order shall
notify the defendant that if he fails to appear and show cause at
the time and place specified by the order the court may order the
sheriff to restore possession of the property to the plaintiff and
may grant such other relief as may be prayed for in the complaint
and provided by this chapter. [1973 1st ex.s. c 207 § 38.]

RCW 59.18.380 Forcible entry or detainer or unlawful detainer
actions--Writ of restitution--Answer--Order--Stay--Bond. At the
time and place fixed for the hearing of plaintiff's motion for a
writ of restitution, the defendant, or any person in possession or
claiming possession of the property, may answer, orally or in
writing, and assert any legal or equitable defense or set-off
arising out of the tenancy. If the answer is oral the substance
thereof shall be endorsed on the complaint by the court. The court
shall examine the parties and witnesses orally to ascertain the
merits of the complaint and answer, and if it shall appear that the
plaintiff has the right to be restored to possession of the
property, the court shall enter an order directing the issuance of
a writ of restitution, returnable ten days after its date,
restoring to the plaintiff possession of the property and if it

shall appear to the court that there is no substantial issue of
material fact of the right of the plaintiff to be granted other
relief as prayed for in the complaint and provided for in this
chapter, the court may enter an order and judgment granting so much
of such relief as may be sustained by the proof, and the court may
grant such other relief as may be prayed for in the plaintiff's
complaint and provided for in this chapter, then the court shall
enter an order denying any relief sought by the plaintiff for which
the court has determined that the plaintiff has no right as a
matter of law: PROVIDED, That within three days after the service
of the writ of restitution the defendant, or person in possession
of the property, may, in any action for the recovery of possession
of the property for failure to pay rent, stay the execution of the
writ pending final judgment by paying into court all rent found to be due and all
the costs of the action, and in addition by paying, on a monthly
basis pending final judgment, an amount equal to the monthly rent
called for by the lease or rental agreement at the time the
complaint was filed: PROVIDED FURTHER, That before any writ shall
issue prior to final judgment the plaintiff shall execute to the
defendant and file in the court a bond in such sum as the court may
order, with sufficient surety to be approved by the clerk,
conditioned that the plaintiff will prosecute his action without
delay, and will pay all costs that may be adjudged to the
defendant, and all damages which he may sustain by reason of the
writ of restitution having been issued, should the same be
wrongfully sued out. The court shall also enter an order directing
the parties to proceed to trial on the complaint and answer in the
usual manner.

If it appears to the court that the plaintiff should not be
restored to possession of the property, the court shall deny
plaintiff's motion for a writ of restitution and enter an order
directing the parties to proceed to trial within thirty days on the
complaint and answer. If it appears to the court that there is a
substantial issue of material fact as to whether or not the
plaintiff is entitled to other relief as is prayed for in
plaintiff's complaint and provided for in this chapter, or that
there is a genuine issue of a material fact pertaining to a legal
or equitable defense or set-off raised in the defendant's answer,
the court shall grant or deny so much of plaintiff's other relief
sought and so much of defendant's defenses or set-off claimed, as
may be proper. [1973 1st ex.s. c 207 § 39.]

RCW 59.18.390 Forcible entry or detainer or unlawful detainer
actions--Writ of restitution--Service--Defendant's bond. (1) The
sheriff shall, upon receiving the writ of restitution, forthwith
serve a copy thereof upon the defendant, his or her agent, or
attorney, or a person in possession of the premises, and shall not
execute the same for three days thereafter, and the defendant, or
person in possession of the premises within three days after the
service of the writ of restitution may execute to the plaintiff a
bond to be filed with and approved by the clerk of the court in
such sum as may be fixed by the judge, with sufficient surety to be
approved by the clerk of the court, conditioned that they will pay
to the plaintiff such sum as the plaintiff may recover for the use
and occupation of the premises, or any rent found due, together
with all damages the plaintiff may sustain by reason of the
defendant occupying or keeping possession of the premises, together
with all damages which the court theretofore has awarded to the

plaintiff as provided in this chapter, and also all the costs of
the action. The plaintiff, his or her agent or attorneys, shall
have notice of the time and place where the court or judge thereof
shall fix the amount of the defendant's bond, and shall have notice
and a reasonable opportunity to examine into the qualification and
sufficiency of the sureties upon the bond before the bond shall be
approved by the clerk. After the issuance of a writ of
restitution, acceptance of a payment by the landlord or plaintiff
that only partially satisfies the judgment will not invalidate the
writ unless pursuant to a written agreement executed by both
parties. The eviction will not be postponed or stopped unless a
copy of that written agreement is provided to the sheriff. It is
the responsibility of the tenant or defendant to ensure a copy of
the agreement is provided to the sheriff. Upon receipt of the
agreement the sheriff will cease action unless ordered to do
otherwise by the court. The writ of restitution and the notice
that accompanies the writ of restitution required under RCW
59.18.312 shall conspicuously state in bold face type, all
capitals, not less than twelve points information about partial
payments as set forth in subsection (2) of this section. If the
writ of restitution has been based upon a finding by the court that
the tenant, subtenant, sublessee, or a person residing at the
rental premises has engaged in drug-related activity or has allowed
any other person to engage in drug-related activity at those
premises with his or her knowledge or approval, neither the tenant,
the defendant, nor a person in possession of the premises shall be
entitled to post a bond in order to retain possession of the
premises. The writ may be served by the sheriff, in the event he
or she shall be unable to find the defendant, an agent or attorney,
or a person in possession of the premises, by affixing a copy of
the writ in a conspicuous place upon the premises: PROVIDED, That
the sheriff shall not require any bond for the service or execution
of the writ. The sheriff shall be immune from all civil liability
for serving and enforcing writs of restitution unless the sheriff
is grossly negligent in carrying out his or her duty.
   (2) The notice accompanying a writ of restitution required
under RCW 59.18.312 shall be substantially similar to the
following:

IMPORTANT NOTICE - PARTIAL PAYMENTS

   YOUR LANDLORD'S ACCEPTANCE OF A PARTIAL PAYMENT FROM YOU AFTER
SERVICE OF THIS WRIT OF RESTITUTION WILL NOT AUTOMATICALLY POSTPONE
OR STOP YOUR EVICTION. IF YOU HAVE A WRITTEN AGREEMENT WITH YOUR
LANDLORD THAT THE EVICTION WILL BE POSTPONED OR STOPPED, IT IS YOUR
RESPONSIBILITY TO PROVIDE A COPY OF THE AGREEMENT TO THE SHERIFF.
THE SHERIFF WILL NOT CEASE ACTION UNLESS YOU PROVIDE A COPY OF THE
AGREEMENT. AT THE DIRECTION OF THE COURT THE SHERIFF MAY TAKE
FURTHER ACTION.

[1997 c 255 § 1; 1989 c 342 § 11; 1988 c 150 § 3; 1973 1st ex.s. c
207 § 40.]

   RCW 59.18.400 Forcible entry or detainer or unlawful detainer
actions--Writ of restitution--Answer of defendant. On or before
the day fixed for his appearance the defendant may appear and
answer. The defendant in his answer may assert any legal or
equitable defense or set-off arising out of the tenancy. If the
complaint alleges that the tenancy should be terminated because the
defendant tenant, subtenant, sublessee, or resident engaged in
drug-related activity, or allowed any other person to engage in
drug-related activity at the rental premises with his or her
knowledge or consent, no set-off shall be allowed as a defense to
the complaint. [1988 c 150 § 4; 1973 1st ex.s. c 207 § 41.]

RCW 59.18.410 Forcible entry or detainer or unlawful detainer actions--Writ of restitution--Judgment--Execution. If upon the trial the verdict of the jury or, if the case be tried without a jury, the finding of the court be in favor of the plaintiff and against the defendant, judgment shall be entered for the restitution of the premises; and if the proceeding be for unlawful detainer after neglect or failure to perform any condition or covenant of a lease or agreement under which the property is held, or after default in the payment of rent, the judgment shall also declare the forfeiture of the lease, agreement or tenancy. The jury, or the court, if the proceedings be tried without a jury, shall also assess the damages arising out of the tenancy occasioned to the plaintiff by any forcible entry, or by any forcible or unlawful detainer, alleged in the complaint and proved on the trial, and, if the alleged unlawful detainer be after default in the payment of rent, find the amount of any rent due, and the judgment shall be rendered against the defendant guilty of the forcible entry, forcible detainer or unlawful detainer for the amount of damages thus assessed and for the rent, if any, found due, and the court may award statutory costs and reasonable attorney's fees. When the proceeding is for an unlawful detainer after default in the payment of rent, and the lease or agreement under which the rent is payable has not by its terms expired, execution upon the judgment shall not be issued until the expiration of five days after the entry of the judgment, within which time the tenant or any subtenant, or any mortgagee of the term, or other party interested in the continuance of the tenancy, may pay into court for the landlord the amount of the judgment and costs, and thereupon the judgment shall be satisfied and the tenant restored to his tenancy; but if payment, as herein provided, be not made within five days the judgment may be enforced for its full amount and for the possession of the premises. In all other cases the judgment may be enforced immediately. If writ of restitution shall have been executed prior to judgment no further writ or execution for the premises shall be required. [1973 1st ex.s. c 207 § 42.]

RCW 59.18.415 Applicability to certain single family dwelling leases. The provisions of this chapter shall not apply to any lease of a single family dwelling for a period of a year or more or to any lease of a single family dwelling containing a bona fide option to purchase by the tenant: PROVIDED, That an attorney for the tenant must approve on the face of the agreement any lease exempted from the provisions of this chapter as provided for in this section. [1989 c 342 § 12; 1973 1st ex.s. c 207 § 43.]

RCW 59.18.420 RCW 59.12.090, 59.12.100, 59.12.121, and 59.12.170 inapplicable. The provisions of RCW 59.12.090, 59.12.100, 59.12.121, and 59.12.170 shall not apply to any rental agreement included under the provisions of chapter 59.18 RCW. [1973 1st ex.s. c 207 § 44.]

RCW 59.18.430 Applicability to prior, existing or future leases. RCW 59.18.010 through 59.18.360 and 59.18.900 shall not apply to any lease entered into prior to July 16, 1973. All provisions of this chapter shall apply to any lease or periodic tenancy entered into on or subsequent to July 16, 1973. [1973 1st ex.s. c 207 § 47.]

RCW 59.18.440 Relocation assistance for low-income tenants--
Certain cities, towns, counties, municipal corporations authorized
to require. (1) Any city, town, county, or municipal corporation
that is required to develop a comprehensive plan under RCW
36.70A.040(1) is authorized to require, after reasonable notice to
the public and a public hearing, property owners to provide their
portion of reasonable relocation assistance to low-income tenants
upon the demolition, substantial rehabilitation whether due to code
enforcement or any other reason, or change of use of residential
property, or upon the removal of use restrictions in an assisted-
housing development. No city, town, county, or municipal
corporation may require property owners to provide relocation
assistance to low-income tenants, as defined in this chapter, upon
the demolition, substantial rehabilitation, upon the change of use
of residential property, or upon the removal of use restrictions in
an assisted-housing development, except as expressly authorized
herein or when authorized or required by state or federal law. As
used in this section, "assisted housing development" means a
multifamily rental housing development that either receives
government assistance and is defined as federally assisted housing
in RCW 59.28.020, or that receives other federal, state, or local
government assistance and is subject to use restrictions.
    (2) As used in this section, "low-income tenants" means
tenants whose combined total income per dwelling unit is at or
below fifty percent of the median income, adjusted for family size,
in the county where the tenants reside.
    The department of community, trade, and economic development
shall adopt rules defining county median income in accordance with
the definitions promulgated by the federal department of housing
and urban development.
    (3) A requirement that property owners provide relocation
assistance shall include the amounts of such assistance to be
provided to low-income tenants. In determining such amounts, the
jurisdiction imposing the requirement shall evaluate, and receive
public testimony on, what relocation expenses displaced tenants
would reasonably incur in that jurisdiction including:
    (a) Actual physical moving costs and expenses;
    (b) Advance payments required for moving into a new residence
such as the cost of first and last month's rent and security and
damage deposits;
    (c) Utility connection fees and deposits; and
    (d) Anticipated additional rent and utility costs in the
residence for one year after relocation.
    (4)(a) Relocation assistance provided to low-income tenants
under this section shall not exceed two thousand dollars for each
dwelling unit displaced by actions of the property owner under
subsection (1) of this section. A city, town, county, or municipal
corporation may make future annual adjustments to the maximum
amount of relocation assistance required under this subsection in
order to reflect any changes in the housing component of the
consumer price index as published by the United States department
of labor, bureau of labor statistics.
    (b) The property owner's portion of any relocation assistance
provided to low-income tenants under this section shall not exceed
one-half of the required relocation assistance under (a) of this
subsection in cash or services.
    (c) The portion of relocation assistance not covered by the
property owner under (b) of this subsection shall be paid by the
city, town, county, or municipal corporation authorized to require
relocation assistance under subsection (1) of this section. The
relocation assistance may be paid from proceeds collected from the

excise tax imposed under RCW 82.46.010.

(5) A city, town, county, or municipal corporation requiring the provision of relocation assistance under this section shall adopt policies, procedures, or regulations to implement such requirement. Such policies, procedures, or regulations shall include provisions for administrative hearings to resolve disputes between tenants and property owners relating to relocation assistance or unlawful detainer actions during relocation, and shall require a decision within thirty days of a request for a hearing by either a tenant or property owner.

Judicial review of an administrative hearing decision relating to relocation assistance may be had by filing a petition, within ten days of the decision, in the superior court in the county where the residential property is located. Judicial review shall be confined to the record of the administrative hearing and the court may reverse the decision only if the administrative findings, inferences, conclusions, or decision is:

(a) In violation of constitutional provisions;

(b) In excess of the authority or jurisdiction of the administrative hearing officer;

(c) Made upon unlawful procedure or otherwise is contrary to law; or

(d) Arbitrary and capricious.

(6) Any city, town, county, or municipal corporation may require relocation assistance, under the terms of this section, for otherwise eligible tenants whose living arrangements are exempted from the provisions of this chapter under RCW 59.18.040(3) and if the living arrangement is considered to be a rental or lease not defined as a retail sale under RCW 82.04.050.

(7)(a) Persons who move from a dwelling unit prior to the application by the owner of the dwelling unit for any governmental permit necessary for the demolition, substantial rehabilitation, or change of use of residential property or prior to any notification or filing required for condominium conversion shall not be entitled to the assistance authorized by this section.

(b) Persons who move into a dwelling unit after the application for any necessary governmental permit or after any required condominium conversion notification or filing shall not be entitled to the assistance authorized by this section if such persons receive written notice from the property owner prior to taking possession of the dwelling unit that specifically describes the activity or condition that may result in their temporary or permanent displacement and advises them of their ineligibility for relocation assistance. [1997 c 452 § 17; 1995 c 399 § 151; 1990 1st ex.s. c 17 § 49.]

RCW 59.18.450 Relocation assistance for low-income tenants-- Payments not considered income--Eligibility for other assistance not affected. Relocation assistance payments received by tenants under *RCW 59.18.440 shall not be considered as income or otherwise affect the eligibility for or amount of assistance paid under any government benefit program. [1990 1st ex.s. c 17 § 50.]

RCW 59.18.500 Gang-related activity--Legislative findings, declarations, and intent. The legislature finds and declares that the ability to feel safe and secure in one's own home and in one's own community is of primary importance. The legislature recognizes that certain gang-related activity can affect the safety of a considerable number of people in the rental premises and dwelling units. Therefore, such activity, although it may be occurring within an individual's home or the surrounding areas of an individual's home, becomes the community's concern.

The legislature intends that the remedy provided in RCW 59.18.510 be used solely to protect the health and safety of the community. The remedy is not a means for private citizens to bring malicious or unfounded actions against fellow tenants or residential neighbors for personal reasons. In determining whether the tenant's activity is the type prohibited under RCW 59.18.130(9), the court should consider the totality of the circumstances, including factors such as whether there have been numerous complaints to the landlord, damage to property, police or incident reports, reports of disturbance, and arrests. An absence of any or all of these factors does not necessarily mean gang activity is not occurring. In determining whether the tenant is engaging in gang-related activity, the court should consider the purpose and intent of RCW 59.18.510. The legislature intends to give people in the community a tool that will help them restore the health and vibrance of their community. [1998 c 276 § 4.]

RCW 59.18.510 Gang-related activity--Notice and demand the landlord commence unlawful detainer action--Petition to court--Attorneys' fees. (1)(a) Any person whose life, safety, health, or use of property is being injured or endangered by a tenant's gang-related activity, who has legal standing and resides, works in, or owns property in the same multifamily building, apartment complex, or within a one-block radius may serve the landlord with a ten-day notice and demand that the landlord commence an unlawful detainer action against the tenant. The notice and demand must set forth, in reasonable detail, facts and circumstances that lead the person to believe gang-related activity is occurring. The notice and demand shall be served by delivering a copy personally to the landlord or the landlord's agent. If the person is unable to personally serve the landlord after exercising due diligence, the person may deposit the notice and demand in the mail, postage prepaid, to the landlord's or the landlord's agent's last known address.

(b) A copy of the notice and demand must also be served upon the tenant engaging in the gang-related activity by delivering a copy personally to the tenant. However, if the person is prevented from personally serving the tenant due to threats or violence, or if personal service is not reasonable under the circumstances, the person may deposit the notice and demand in the mail, postage prepaid, to the tenant's address, or leave a copy of the notice and demand in a conspicuous location at the tenant's residence.

(2)(a) Within ten days from the time the notice and demand is served, the landlord has a duty to take reasonable steps to investigate the tenant's alleged noncompliance with RCW 59.18.130(9). The landlord must notify the person who brought the notice and demand that an investigation is occurring. The landlord has ten days from the time he or she notifies the person in which to conduct a reasonable investigation.

(b) If, after reasonable investigation, the landlord finds that the tenant is not in compliance with RCW 59.18.130(9), the landlord may proceed directly to an unlawful detainer action or take reasonable steps to ensure the tenant discontinues the prohibited activity and complies with RCW 59.18.130(9). The landlord shall notify the person who served the notice and demand of whatever action the landlord takes.

(c) If, after reasonable investigation, the landlord finds that the tenant is in compliance with RCW 59.18.130(9), the landlord shall notify the person who served the notice and demand of the landlord's findings.

(3) The person who served the notice and demand may petition the appropriate court to have the tenancy terminated and the tenant removed from the premises if: (a) Within ten days of service of the notice and demand, the tenant fails to discontinue the gang-related activity and the landlord fails to conduct a reasonable investigation; or (b) the landlord notifies the person that the landlord conducted a reasonable investigation and found that the tenant was not engaged in gang-related activity as prohibited under RCW 59.18.130(9); or (c) the landlord took reasonable steps to have the tenant comply with RCW 59.18.130(9), but the tenant has failed to comply within a reasonable time.

(4) If the court finds that the tenant was not in compliance with RCW 59.18.130(9), the court shall enter an order terminating the tenancy and requiring the tenant to vacate the premises. The court shall not issue the order terminating the tenancy unless it has found that the allegations of gang-related activity are corroborated by a source other than the person who has petitioned the court.

(5) The prevailing party shall recover reasonable attorneys' fees and costs. The court may impose sanctions, in addition to attorneys' fees, on a person who has brought an action under this chapter against the same tenant on more than one occasion, if the court finds the petition was brought with the intent to harass. However, the court must order the landlord to pay costs and reasonable attorneys' fees to the person petitioning for termination of the tenancy if the court finds that the landlord failed to comply with the duty to investigate, regardless of which party prevails. [1998 c 276 § 5.]

RCW 59.18.900 Severability--1973 1st ex.s. c 207. If any provision of this chapter, or its application to any person or circumstance is held invalid, the remainder of the act, or its application to other persons or circumstances, is not affected. [1973 1st ex.s. c 207 § 37.]

RCW 59.18.910 Severability--1989 c 342. If any provision of this act or its application to any person or circumstance is held invalid, the remainder of the act or the application of the provision to other persons or circumstances is not affected. [1989 c 342 § 18.]

RCW 59.18.911 Effective date--1989 c 342. This act shall take effect on August 1, 1989, and shall apply to landlord-tenant relationships existing on or entered into after the effective date of this act. [1989 c 342 § 19.]